C++ for Robotic Development with OpenCV and ROS

**A Hands-on Guide to Building Robotics
Applications with OpenCV and ROS**

Jade L. Rhodes

Table of contents

Part I: Foundations of C++ for Robotics

Chapter 1. Introduction to C++ for Robotics

This chapter lays the foundation for understanding why C++ is a powerful and widely adopted language in the field of robotics. We will explore its key features, trace its historical evolution, and provide a step-by-step guide to setting up a robust development environment.

1.1 Overview of C++ and its Relevance to Robotics

C++ is a general-purpose programming language known for its performance, flexibility, and control over system resources. These characteristics make it exceptionally well-suited for robotics applications, which often demand real-time processing, efficient memory management, and direct hardware interaction.

Key Features of C++ Relevant to Robotics:

- Performance: C++ compiles directly to machine code, resulting in fast execution speeds. This is crucial for real-time control systems in robots, where delays can lead to instability or failure.
- Low-Level Control: C++ allows direct access to hardware through pointers and memory management, enabling precise control over sensors, actuators, and other robotic components.
- Object-Oriented Programming (OOP): OOP principles like encapsulation, inheritance, and polymorphism facilitate the development of modular, reusable, and maintainable code. This is essential for managing the complexity of robotic systems.
- Standard Template Library (STL): The STL provides a rich set of data structures and algorithms, simplifying common

programming tasks and improving code efficiency.

- Extensive Libraries: Numerous libraries, such as ROS (Robot Operating System) and OpenCV (Open Source Computer Vision Library), are built upon C++, providing pre-built functionalities for robotics applications.
- Real-time Capabilities: C++ is often used in conjunction with Real-Time Operating Systems (RTOS) to ensure deterministic execution, which is critical for safety-critical robotic systems.
- Cross-Platform Compatibility: C++ code can be compiled and run on various platforms, including embedded systems, desktop computers, and servers, making it versatile for diverse robotic applications.

Why C++ is Essential for Robotics:

- Real-time Control: Robots often need to react to sensor data and execute commands in real-time. C++'s performance and low-level control make it ideal for these applications.

- Hardware Interfacing: Robots interact with a variety of hardware components, including sensors, motors, and communication devices. C++'s ability to directly access hardware enables seamless integration.
- Complex Algorithms: Robotics often involves complex algorithms for navigation, perception, and control. C++'s powerful features and libraries facilitate the implementation of these algorithms.
- Embedded Systems: Many robotic systems rely on embedded systems with limited resources. C++'s efficiency and memory management capabilities make it suitable for these environments.
- Industry Standard: C++ is widely used in the robotics industry, ensuring compatibility with existing systems and a large pool of experienced developers.

1.2 Brief History of C++ and its Evolution

C++ evolved from the C programming language, which was developed at Bell Labs in the early 1970s. Bjarne Stroustrup began working on "C with Classes" in 1979, adding object-oriented features to C. This evolved into C++, standardized by the International Organization for Standardization (ISO).

Key Milestones in C++ History:

- 1979: C with Classes: Bjarne Stroustrup began developing "C with Classes" to add object-oriented features to C.
- 1983: C++: "C with Classes" was renamed C++.
- 1985: First Commercial Release: The first commercial release of C++ was made available.
- 1998: C++98 (ISO/IEC 14882:1998): The first ISO standard for C++ was published, defining the core language and the STL.
- 2003: C++03 (ISO/IEC 14882:2003): A minor revision of C++98, addressing defects and inconsistencies.

- 2011: C++11 (ISO/IEC 14882:2011): A major revision introducing significant new features, including lambda expressions, auto type deduction, and move semantics.
- 2014: C++14 (ISO/IEC 14882:2014): A minor revision building upon C++11, adding features like generic lambda expressions and binary literals.
- 2017: C++17 (ISO/IEC 14882:2017): A major revision introducing features like structured bindings, inline variables, and parallel algorithms.
- 2020: C++20 (ISO/IEC 14882:2020): A major revision introducing concepts, ranges, coroutines, and modules.
- 2023: C++23 (ISO/IEC 14882:2023): Includes features like deducing this, if consteval, and enhancements to ranges.

Evolution and Modern C++:

Modern C++ (C++11 and later) has significantly improved the language's usability and expressiveness. The introduction of features like smart pointers, lambda expressions, and move semantics has made C++ safer and more efficient. The ongoing evolution of C++ ensures that it remains a powerful and relevant language for robotics development.

1.3 Setting up the Development Environment

To begin developing robotics applications with C++, you need to set up a suitable development environment. This typically involves installing a compiler, an IDE (Integrated Development Environment) or a text editor, and any necessary libraries.

Steps to Set up the Development Environment:

1. Choose a Compiler:
   o GCC (GNU Compiler Collection): A popular and widely used open-source compiler, available for various platforms.
   o Clang: A modern and efficient compiler known for its excellent error messages.

- MSVC (Microsoft Visual C++): The compiler included in Microsoft Visual Studio, suitable for Windows development.
2. Install a Compiler:
    - Windows: Download and install MSVC from the Visual Studio website or use MinGW or WSL (Windows Subsystem for Linux) to install GCC or Clang.
    - macOS: Install Xcode from the App Store, which includes Clang. Alternatively, install Homebrew and then install GCC or Clang.
    - Linux: Use your distribution's package manager to install GCC or Clang (e.g., sudo apt-get install g++ on Ubuntu/Debian).
3. Choose an IDE or Text Editor:
    - Visual Studio Code (VS Code): A lightweight and highly extensible code editor with excellent C++ support.

- CLion: A powerful IDE specifically designed for C++ development.
- Qt Creator: an IDE that is often used with the Qt framework, which is frequently used in robotics projects.
- Eclipse CDT (C/C++ Development Tooling): A feature-rich IDE with extensive C++ support.
- Vim/Emacs: Highly configurable text editors for experienced developers.

4. Install Necessary Libraries:
   - ROS (Robot Operating System): A widely used framework for robotics development. Installation instructions are available on the ROS website.
   - OpenCV (Open Source Computer Vision Library): A library for computer vision applications, often used in robotics. Installation instructions are available on the OpenCV website.

- Eigen: a c++ template library for linear algebra. Used in many Robotics applications.
- PCL (Point Cloud Library): A library for 3D point cloud processing, used in robotics for perception and navigation.

5. Configure the IDE/Editor:
   - Configure the IDE or editor to use the installed compiler.
   - Install necessary extensions or plugins for C++ development.
   - Set up debugging tools for easier troubleshooting.

6. Verify the Installation:
   - Write a simple "Hello, World!" program to ensure that the compiler and IDE/editor are working correctly.
   - Compile and run the program to verify the setup.

Example "Hello, World!" Program:

C++

```cpp
#include <iostream>

int main() {
    std::cout << "Hello, World!" << std::endl;
    return 0;
}
```

This comprehensive introduction provides a solid foundation for delving into C++ programming for robotics. By understanding the language's strengths, its historical context, and how to set up a development environment, you are well-equipped to embark on your robotics development journey.

Chapter 2. C++ Fundamentals for Robotics

This chapter delves into the fundamental concepts of C++ programming, providing the essential building blocks for developing robust and efficient robotics applications. We will cover variables, data types, operators, control structures, functions, arrays, and the core principles of Object-Oriented Programming (OOP).

2.1 Variables, Data Types, and Operators

Variables are named storage locations in memory that hold data. Data types define the kind of data a variable can store, and operators are symbols that perform operations on variables and values.

Variables:

- Declaration: Variables must be declared before they can be used. The declaration specifies the variable's data type and name.
  - Example: int count; float temperature;
- Initialization: Variables can be initialized when they are declared, assigning them an initial value.
  - Example: int count = 0; float temperature = 25.5;
- Scope: The scope of a variable determines where it can be accessed within the program.

Data Types:

- Primitive Data Types:
  - int: Integer numbers (e.g., -10, 0, 100).
  - float: Single-precision floating-point numbers (e.g., 3.14, -2.5).

- o double: Double-precision floating-point numbers (e.g., 3.14159, -2.71828).
  - o char: Single characters (e.g., 'a', 'Z', '9').
  - o bool: Boolean values (true or false).
- Modifiers:
  - o signed: Can store positive and negative values.
  - o unsigned: Can store only non-negative values.
  - o short: A smaller integer type.
  - o long: A larger integer type.
  - o long long: An even larger integer type.
- Derived Data Types:
  - o Arrays, pointers, structures, unions, classes, and enumerations.

Operators:

- Arithmetic Operators:

- + (addition), - (subtraction), * (multiplication), / (division), % (modulo).
- Assignment Operators:
  - = (assignment), +=, -=, *=, /=, %=.
-
- Comparison Operators:
  - == (equal to), != (not equal to), > (greater than), < (less than), >= (greater than or equal to), <= (less than or equal[1] to).
-
- Logical Operators:
  - && (logical AND), || (logical OR), ! (logical NOT).
-
- Bitwise Operators:
  - & (bitwise AND), | (bitwise OR), ^ (bitwise XOR), ~ (bitwise NOT), << (left shift), >> (right shift).[2]
- Increment and Decrement Operators:
  - ++ (increment), -- (decrement).
- Conditional Operator (Ternary Operator):

- condition ? expression1 : expression2.

2.2 Control Structures, Functions, and Arrays

Control structures dictate the flow of execution in a program. Functions encapsulate reusable blocks of code, and arrays store collections of elements of the same data type.

Control Structures:

- Conditional Statements:
    - if statement: Executes a block of code if a condition is true.
    - if-else statement: Executes one block of code if a condition is true and another block if it is false.
    - if-else if-else statement: Executes different blocks of code based on multiple conditions.
    - switch statement: Executes different blocks of code based on the value of an expression.
- Looping Statements:

- for loop: Executes a block of code a specified number of times.
- while loop: Executes a block of code while a condition is true.
- do-while loop: Executes a block of code at least once[4] and then continues while a condition is true.

- Jump Statements:
  - break: Terminates a loop or switch statement.
  - continue: Skips the current iteration of a loop.
  - return: Exits a function and returns a value.
  - goto: Transfers control to a labeled statement (generally discouraged).

Functions:

- Function Declaration: Specifies the function's name, return type, and parameters.
  - Example: int add(int a, int b);

- Function Definition: Provides the implementation of the function.
  - Example: int add(int a, int b) { return a + b; }
- Function Call: Executes the function.
  - Example: int sum = add(5, 10);
- Function Parameters: Input values passed to a function.
- Return Value: The value returned by a function.
- Function Overloading: Defining multiple functions with the same name but different parameters.

Arrays:

- Declaration: Specifies the array's data type and size.
  - Example: int numbers[5];
- Initialization: Assigning initial values to array elements.
  - Example: int numbers[5] = {1, 2, 3, 4, 5};

- Accessing Elements: Accessing individual elements using their index (starting from 0).
  - Example: numbers[0] = 10;
- Multidimensional Arrays: Arrays with multiple dimensions.
  - Example: int matrix[3][3];
- Pointers and Arrays: Arrays can be accessed using pointers.

2.3 Object-Oriented Programming (OOP) Concepts

OOP is a programming paradigm that organizes code around objects, which are instances of classes.[5] OOP promotes code reusability, maintainability, and modularity.

Key OOP Concepts:

- Classes: Blueprints for creating objects. A class defines the attributes (data members) and behaviors (member functions) of its objects.
  - Example:

- C++

```cpp
class Robot {
public:
    int id;
    void move();
};
```

-
-

- Objects: Instances of a class. Objects have their own set of attributes and can perform the behaviors defined by their class.
  - Example: Robot robot1;
- Encapsulation: Bundling data and methods that operate on the data within a single unit (class). This hides the internal details of an object and protects its data from unauthorized access.
- Inheritance: Creating new classes (derived classes) from existing classes (base classes). Derived classes inherit the attributes and behaviors of their base classes and can add or modify them.

- ○ Example:
- ○ C++

```
class WheeledRobot : public Robot {
public:
    int numberOfWheels;
};
```

- ○
- ○
- Polymorphism: The ability of objects of different classes to respond to the same method call in different ways. This allows[6] for flexibility and code reusability.
  - ○ Compile-time Polymorphism (Function Overloading and Operator Overloading): Determining which function or operator to call at compile time.
  - ○ Run-time Polymorphism (Virtual Functions): Determining which method to call at runtime, based on the object's actual type.
-

- Abstraction: Hiding complex implementation details and exposing only the essential features of an object. This simplifies the use of objects and reduces complexity.
- Constructors: Special member functions that initialize objects when they are created.
- Destructors: Special member functions that clean up resources when objects are destroyed.
- Access Specifiers:
  - public: Members can be accessed from anywhere.
  - private: Members can be accessed only within the class.
  - protected: Members can be accessed within the class and its derived classes.

These C++ fundamentals are crucial for building complex robotic systems. Mastering these concepts will enable you to write efficient, maintainable, and scalable code for various robotics applications.

Chapter 3. C++ Standard Template Library (STL) for Robotics

This chapter explores the C++ Standard Template Library (STL), a powerful collection of template classes and functions that provide ready-to-use data structures and algorithms. The STL significantly simplifies and accelerates the development of robotics applications by offering efficient and reusable components.

3.1 Introduction to the STL and its Relevance to Robotics

The STL is a cornerstone of modern C++ programming, providing a set of generic classes and functions that can be used with any data type. It consists of three main components: containers, algorithms, and iterators.

Key Components of the STL:

- Containers: Template classes that implement common data structures, such as vectors, lists, maps, and sets.
- Algorithms: Template functions that perform common operations on data, such as sorting, searching, and transforming.
- Iterators: Objects that provide a way to access elements in containers.

Relevance of the STL to Robotics:

- Efficient Data Management: Robots often deal with large amounts of data from sensors and other sources. STL containers provide efficient ways to store and manipulate this data.
- Algorithm Implementation: Robotics algorithms, such as path planning and sensor fusion, can be implemented using STL algorithms, reducing development time and improving code quality.
- Code Reusability: The STL promotes code reusability, allowing developers to focus on the specific requirements of their robotics applications.

- Performance Optimization: The STL is designed for performance, providing optimized implementations of common data structures and algorithms.
- Standardization: Using the STL ensures that code is portable and compatible with other C++ libraries and tools.

3.2 Using STL Containers, Algorithms, and Iterators

This section explores the practical application of STL components in robotics development.

STL Containers:

- std::vector: A dynamic array that can grow or shrink in size. Ideal for storing sequences of elements that need to be accessed randomly.
  - Example: Storing sensor readings, waypoints for navigation.
- C++

```
#include <vector>
```

```cpp
#include <iostream>

int main() {
    std::vector<double> sensorReadings;
    sensorReadings.push_back(1.5);
    sensorReadings.push_back(2.8);
    for (double reading : sensorReadings) {
        std::cout << reading << " ";
    }
    std::cout << std::endl;
    return 0;
}
```

-
-
- std::list: A doubly linked list that allows efficient insertion and deletion of elements at any position. Ideal for tasks involving frequent modifications to the data structure.
    - Example: Managing a queue of tasks, implementing a circular buffer.
- std::deque: A double-ended queue that allows efficient insertion and deletion at

both ends. Ideal for implementing queues and stacks.

- std::map: An associative container that stores key-value pairs, where keys are unique and sorted. Ideal for storing mappings between data, such as sensor IDs and their corresponding values.
  - Example: Storing robot configurations, mapping object IDs to their properties.
- C++

```cpp
#include <map>
#include <iostream>

int main() {
    std::map<std::string, double> robotConfig;
    robotConfig["speed"] = 10.0;
    robotConfig["rotation"] = 90.0;
    std::cout << "Speed: " << robotConfig["speed"] << std::endl;
    return 0;
}
```

-
-
- std::set: A sorted collection of unique elements. Ideal for storing sets of data, such as detected objects.
  - Example: Keeping track of unique obstacles in a map.
- std::unordered_map and std::unordered_set: Hash-based containers that provide fast lookups, insertions, and deletions. Ideal when order is not important, but speed is.

STL Algorithms:

- std::sort: Sorts the elements in a range.
  - Example: Sorting sensor readings, sorting a list of detected objects.
- std::find: Searches for an element in a range.
  - Example: Finding a specific object in a list of detected objects.
- std::transform: Applies a function to each element in a range.

- Example: Scaling sensor readings, converting data to a different format.
- std::accumulate: Computes the sum of elements in a range.
  - Example: Calculating the average of sensor readings.
- std::copy: Copies elements from one range to another.
  - Example: Copying sensor data to a buffer.
- std::for_each: Applies a function to each element in a range.
- std::count: Counts the number of occurrences of an element in a range.

STL Iterators:

- Iterators provide a way to traverse the elements in a container.
- They abstract the underlying data structure, allowing algorithms to work with different types of containers.
- Types of iterators: input, output, forward, bidirectional, and random access.

- Example: Using iterators to traverse a vector.
- C++

```cpp
#include <vector>
#include <iostream>

int main() {
    std::vector<int> numbers = {1, 2, 3, 4, 5};
        for (std::vector<int>::iterator it =
numbers.begin(); it != numbers.end(); ++it) {
        std::cout << *it << " ";
    }
    std::cout << std::endl;
    return 0;
}
}
```

-
-
- Range-based for loops, introduced in C++11, often make the usage of iterators implicit and easier.

```cpp
#include <vector>

#include <iostream>

int main() {
    std::vector<int> numbers = {1, 2, 3, 4, 5};
    for (int number : numbers) {
        std::cout << number << " ";
    }
    std::cout << std::endl;
    return 0;
}
}
```

By mastering the STL, robotics developers can write efficient, maintainable, and reusable code, significantly accelerating the development process. The STL provides powerful tools for managing data, implementing algorithms, and working with various data structures, making it an indispensable part of C++ programming for robotics.

Part II: Computer Vision with OpenCV

Chapter 4. Introduction to OpenCV and Computer Vision

This chapter introduces OpenCV (Open Source Computer Vision Library), a powerful and widely used library for computer vision tasks, and explores the fundamental concepts of computer vision. We will also cover the essential steps to set up OpenCV with C++ for robotics applications.

4.1 Overview of OpenCV and its Features

OpenCV is a cross-platform library that provides a comprehensive set of tools for computer vision, image processing, and machine learning. Its versatility and efficiency make it an indispensable resource for robotics developers working on perception and navigation systems.

Key Features of OpenCV:

- Image Processing: OpenCV provides a wide range of functions for image manipulation, including filtering, transformations, color space conversions, and geometric operations.
- Video Analysis: OpenCV supports video processing tasks such as motion detection, object tracking, and video stabilization.
- Object Detection: OpenCV includes algorithms for detecting objects in images and videos, such as face detection, pedestrian detection, and object recognition.
- Machine Learning: OpenCV integrates with machine learning libraries and provides tools for training and deploying machine learning models for computer vision tasks.
- Camera Calibration and 3D Reconstruction: OpenCV offers functions for calibrating cameras and reconstructing 3D scenes from multiple images.
- Feature Detection and Matching: OpenCV provides algorithms for detecting and

matching features in images, which are essential for tasks like image stitching and object recognition.

- Graphical User Interface (GUI): OpenCV includes functions for creating simple GUIs for displaying images and videos.
- Cross-Platform Compatibility: OpenCV runs on various platforms, including Windows, macOS, Linux, and embedded systems.
- Open Source: OpenCV is an open-source library, making it freely available for use in both commercial and non-commercial applications.
- C++, Python, and Java Interfaces: OpenCV provides interfaces for multiple programming languages, including C++, Python, and Java.

Relevance to Robotics:

- Perception: Robots rely on computer vision to perceive their environment. OpenCV enables robots to process images and videos from cameras and other sensors, extracting relevant information about their surroundings.

- Navigation: Computer vision is essential for robot navigation, allowing robots to detect obstacles, recognize landmarks, and follow paths.
- Object Recognition: OpenCV enables robots to recognize and identify objects in their environment, which is crucial for tasks like object manipulation and autonomous navigation.
- Human-Robot Interaction: Computer vision can be used to enable robots to interact with humans, such as recognizing gestures and facial expressions.
- Sensor Fusion: OpenCV can be used to fuse data from multiple sensors, such as cameras and lidar, to create a more complete understanding of the environment.

4.2 Basic Concepts of Computer Vision

Computer vision involves the development of algorithms and techniques that enable computers to "see" and interpret images and videos. Understanding the basic concepts of computer vision is essential for working with OpenCV.

Key Concepts:

- Image Representation: Images are typically represented as arrays of pixels, where each pixel stores color information.
- Image Processing: Image processing involves manipulating images to enhance their quality, extract features, or perform other operations.
- Feature Detection: Feature detection involves identifying distinctive points or regions in an image that can be used for tasks like object recognition and image matching.
- Feature Matching: Feature matching involves finding corresponding features in two or more images.

- Object Detection: Object detection involves identifying and locating objects in an image or video.
- Image Segmentation: Image segmentation involves partitioning an image into multiple segments or regions.
- Camera Calibration: Camera calibration involves determining the intrinsic and extrinsic parameters of a camera.
- 3D Reconstruction: 3D reconstruction involves creating a 3D model of a scene from multiple images.
- Machine Learning in Computer Vision: Machine learning techniques, such as deep learning, are increasingly used in computer vision tasks.
- Color Spaces: Different ways of representing color, such as RGB (Red, Green, Blue), HSV (Hue, Saturation, Value), and grayscale.
- Image Filtering: Techniques for modifying pixel values to achieve effects like blurring, sharpening, or noise reduction.

- Geometric Transformations: Operations that alter the spatial arrangement of pixels, such as rotation, translation, and scaling.

4.3 Setting up OpenCV with C++

To use OpenCV with C++, you need to install the library and configure your development environment.

Steps to Set up OpenCV with C++:

1. Download OpenCV:
   - Download the latest stable release of OpenCV from the official OpenCV website.
   - Choose the appropriate version for your operating system and compiler.
2. Install OpenCV:
   - Windows: Extract the downloaded archive to a directory of your choice. Configure system environment variables to include OpenCV's bin folder.

- macOS: Use Homebrew to install OpenCV: brew install opencv.
- Linux: Use your distribution's package manager: sudo apt-get install libopencv-dev (Ubuntu/Debian).

3. Configure Your IDE/Build System:
- Visual Studio Code (VS Code): Create a tasks.json file to configure the compiler and linker settings.
- CLion: Configure the CMakeLists.txt file to link the OpenCV libraries.
- CMake: Create a CMakeLists.txt file to specify the OpenCV libraries and include directories.

4. Create a Simple OpenCV Project:
- Create a new C++ project in your IDE or build system.
- Write a simple program to load and display an image.

Example OpenCV Program (Loading and Displaying an Image):

C++

```cpp
#include <iostream>
#include <opencv2/opencv.hpp>

int main(int argc, char** argv) {
    if (argc != 2) {
        std::cout << "Usage: display_image <image_path>" << std::endl;
        return -1;
    }

    cv::Mat image = cv::imread(argv[1], cv::IMREAD_COLOR);

    if (image.empty()) {
        std::cout << "Could not open or find the image" << std::endl;
        return -1;
    }

    cv::imshow("Display window", image);
```

```cpp
cv::waitKey(0);

    return 0;
}
```

5. Compile and Run the Program:
   - Compile the program using your IDE or build system.
   - Run the program, passing the path to an image file as a command-line argument.

This setup provides a foundation for developing computer vision applications with OpenCV in C++. By mastering these concepts and techniques, you can enable robots to perceive and interact with their environment in sophisticated ways.

Chapter 5. Image Processing with OpenCV

This chapter delves into the practical aspects of image processing using OpenCV, a crucial skill for robotics developers. We will explore how to read and write images, apply various filtering and thresholding techniques, and perform image transformations and feature detection.

5.1 Reading and Writing Images

The first step in any image processing task is to read and write images. OpenCV provides convenient functions for handling various image formats.

Reading Images:

- cv::imread(): This function reads an image from a file and returns a cv::Mat object, which is OpenCV's matrix class for storing image data.

- o Syntax: cv::Mat cv::imread(const String& filename, int flags = cv::IMREAD_COLOR);
- o filename: The path to the image file.
- o flags: Specifies the color type of the loaded image.
  - cv::IMREAD_COLOR: Loads a color image.
  - cv::IMREAD_GRAYSCALE : Loads a grayscale image.
  - cv::IMREAD_UNCHANGED: Loads the image as is, including the alpha channel.
- o Example:
- o C++

```
#include <opencv2/opencv.hpp>
#include <iostream>

int main() {
```

```
    cv::Mat image = cv::imread("image.jpg",
cv::IMREAD_COLOR);
    if (image.empty()) {
        std::cerr << "Error: Could not open or find
the image." << std::endl;
        return -1;
    }
    cv::imshow("Loaded Image", image);
    cv::waitKey(0);
    return 0;
}
```

      ○

      ○

Writing Images:

- cv::imwrite(): This function writes an image to a file.
    - **Syntax**: bool cv::imwrite(const String& filename, InputArray img, const std::vector<int>& params = std::vector<int>());
    - filename: The path to the output image file.

- img: The input image (cv::Mat object).
- params: Optional parameters for specific image formats (e.g., JPEG quality).
- Example:
- C++

```cpp
#include <opencv2/opencv.hpp>
#include <iostream>

int main() {
    cv::Mat image = cv::imread("image.jpg", cv::IMREAD_COLOR);
    if (image.empty()) {
        std::cerr << "Error: Could not open or find the image." << std::endl;
        return -1;
    }
    cv::imwrite("output.png", image);
    return 0;
}
```

-

o

5.2 Image Filtering and Thresholding

Image filtering and thresholding are essential techniques for enhancing images, removing noise, and segmenting objects.

Image Filtering:

- Blurring:
  - cv::blur(): Applies a simple average filter to blur an image.
  - cv::GaussianBlur(): Applies a Gaussian filter for more effective blurring.
  - cv::medianBlur(): Applies a median filter, useful for removing salt-and-pepper noise.
  - Example:
  - C++

```
#include <opencv2/opencv.hpp>
```

```
int main() {
    cv::Mat  image  =  cv::imread("image.jpg",
cv::IMREAD_COLOR);
    cv::Mat blurredImage;
        cv::GaussianBlur(image,  blurredImage,
cv::Size(5, 5), 0);
    cv::imshow("Blurred Image", blurredImage);
    cv::waitKey(0);
    return 0;
}
```

   ○

   ○

- Sharpening: Applying custom kernels to enhance edges and details.
- Edge Detection:
   ○ cv::Sobel(): Computes the first derivative of an image, highlighting edges.
   ○ cv::Laplacian(): Computes the second derivative of an image, highlighting edges.

- cv::Canny(): A multi-stage edge detection algorithm that is highly effective.

Image Thresholding:

- cv::threshold(): Converts a grayscale image to a binary image based on a threshold value.
  - Syntax: double cv::threshold(InputArray src, OutputArray dst, double thresh, double maxval, int type);
  - src: The input grayscale image.
  - dst: The output binary image.
  - thresh: The threshold value.
  - maxval: The maximum value to use with the cv::THRESH_BINARY and cv::THRESH_BINARY_INV types.
  - type: The thresholding type.
    - cv::THRESH_BINARY: If pixel > threshold, pixel = maxval; otherwise, pixel = 0.

- cv::THRESH_BINARY_INV
  : Inverted binary thresholding.
- cv::THRESH_TRUNC: If pixel > threshold, pixel = threshold; otherwise, pixel = pixel.
- cv::THRESH_TOZERO: If pixel > threshold, pixel = pixel; otherwise, pixel = 0.
- cv::THRESH_TOZERO_INV: Inverted to zero thresholding.
- Example:
- C++

```cpp
#include <opencv2/opencv.hpp>

int main() {
    cv::Mat image = cv::imread("image.jpg", cv::IMREAD_GRAYSCALE);
    cv::Mat thresholdedImage;
```

```cpp
    cv::threshold(image, thresholdedImage, 127,
255, cv::THRESH_BINARY);
            cv::imshow("Thresholded    Image",
thresholdedImage);
    cv::waitKey(0);
    return 0;
}
```

   o

   o

- cv::adaptiveThreshold(): Calculates the threshold value for each pixel based on a small region around it.

5.3 Image Transformations and Feature Detection

Image transformations and feature detection are essential for tasks like object recognition, image stitching, and 3D reconstruction.

Image Transformations:

- Geometric Transformations:
   o cv::resize(): Resizes an image.

- ○ cv::warpAffine(): Applies an affine transformation (rotation, translation, scaling).
- ○ cv::warpPerspective(): Applies a perspective transformation.
- ○ cv::rotate(): Rotates an image by 90, 180, or 270 degrees.
- Color Space Conversions:
  - ○ cv::cvtColor(): Converts an image from one color space to another (e.g., RGB to grayscale, RGB to HSV).

Feature Detection:

- Corner Detection:
  - ○ cv::cornerHarris(): Detects corners using the Harris corner detection algorithm.
  - ○ cv::goodFeaturesToTrack(): Detects strong corners for tracking.
- Feature Descriptors:
  - ○ SIFT (Scale-Invariant Feature Transform): Detects and describes

local features that are invariant to scale and rotation. (Non free)
- SURF (Speeded-Up Robust Features): A faster version of SIFT. (Non free)
- ORB (Oriented FAST and Rotated BRIEF): A fast and efficient feature detector and descriptor.
- BRISK (Binary Robust Invariant Scalable Keypoints): Another fast and efficient feature detector and descriptor.
- AKAZE (Accelerated-KAZE): A nonlinear scale space feature detector and descriptor.
- Feature Matching:
  - cv::BFMatcher: Brute-force matcher.
  - cv::FlannBasedMatcher: Fast Library for Approximate Nearest Neighbors matcher.
  - Example (ORB Feature Detection and Matching):
  - C++

```cpp
#include <opencv2/opencv.hpp>
#include <iostream>

int main() {
    cv::Mat image1 = cv::imread("image1.jpg",
cv::IMREAD_GRAYSCALE);
    cv::Mat image2 = cv::imread("image2.jpg",
cv::IMREAD_GRAYSCALE);

    std::vector<cv::KeyPoint> keypoints1,
keypoints2;
    cv::Mat descriptors1, descriptors2;

    cv::Ptr<cv::ORB> orb = cv::ORB::create();
    orb->detectAndCompute(image1, cv::Mat(),
keypoints1, descriptors1);
    orb->detectAndCompute(image2, cv::Mat(),
keypoints2, descriptors2);

    cv::BFMatcher
matcher(cv::NORM_HAMMING);
    std::vector<cv::DMatch> matches;
    matcher.match(descriptors1, descriptors2,
matches);
```

```
cv::Mat matchedImage;
        cv::drawMatches(image1,  keypoints1,
image2, keypoints2, matches, matchedImage);
            cv::imshow("Matched   Features",
matchedImage);
    cv::waitKey(0);
    return 0;
}
```

○

○

These image processing techniques are
fundamental for enabling robots to perceive and
interpret their environment. By mastering these
skills, robotics developers can create
sophisticated perception systems for various
applications.

Chapter 6. Object Detection and Tracking with OpenCV

This chapter explores the essential techniques of object detection and tracking using OpenCV, which are fundamental for enabling robots to perceive and interact with dynamic environments. We will cover Haar cascades, feature detectors, Kalman filters, and particle filters.

6.1 Introduction to Object Detection and Tracking

Object detection involves identifying and locating objects of interest within an image or video frame. Object tracking, on the other hand, involves following the movement of a detected object over time. These techniques are crucial for various robotics applications, including autonomous navigation, object manipulation, and human-robot interaction.

Object Detection:

- Goal: To identify the presence and location of specific objects within an image or video frame.
- Methods:
  - Haar cascades
  - Feature detectors (SIFT, SURF, ORB, etc.)
  - Deep learning-based object detectors (YOLO, SSD, Faster R-CNN)
- Applications:
  - Face detection
  - Pedestrian detection
  - Object recognition
  - Obstacle detection

Object Tracking:

- Goal: To follow the movement of a detected object over time.

- Methods:
  - Kalman filters
  - Particle filters
  - Mean shift tracking
  - Optical flow
  - Correlation tracking
- Applications:
  - Robot navigation
  - Motion analysis
  - Video surveillance
  - Human-robot interaction

6.2 Using Haar Cascades and Feature Detectors

Haar cascades and feature detectors are traditional methods for object detection, offering a balance between performance and computational cost.

Haar Cascades:

- Concept: Haar cascades are machine learning-based object detectors that use Haar-like features to identify objects.
- Process:

- Haar-like features are rectangular features that capture differences in pixel intensities.
- A cascade of classifiers is trained on a large dataset of positive and negative images.
- The cascade is applied to an image, and if a region passes all stages of the cascade, it is classified as an object.
- Advantages:
  - Relatively fast and efficient.
  - Suitable for real-time applications.
- Disadvantages:
  - Sensitive to variations in lighting, scale, and orientation.
  - Limited to detecting specific object classes for which cascades are trained.
- OpenCV Implementation:
  - cv::CascadeClassifier: Class for loading and using Haar cascades.
  - cv::detectMultiScale(): Function for detecting objects in an image.

- Example:
- C++

```cpp
#include <opencv2/opencv.hpp>
#include <iostream>

int main() {
    cv::CascadeClassifier faceCascade;
    if (!faceCascade.load("haarcascade_frontalface_default.xml")) {
        std::cerr << "Error loading face cascade." << std::endl;
        return -1;
    }

    cv::Mat image = cv::imread("faces.jpg");
    std::vector<cv::Rect> faces;
    faceCascade.detectMultiScale(image, faces, 1.1, 3, 0 | cv::CASCADE_SCALE_IMAGE, cv::Size(30, 30));

    for (const auto& face : faces) {
```

```cpp
    cv::rectangle(image, face, cv::Scalar(255, 0,
0), 2);
    }

    cv::imshow("Detected Faces", image);
    cv::waitKey(0);
    return 0;
}
```
○
○

Feature Detectors:

- Concept: Feature detectors identify
  distinctive points or regions in an image,
  which can be used for object detection and
  matching.
- Methods:
  - SIFT (Scale-Invariant Feature
    Transform)
  - SURF (Speeded-Up Robust
    Features)
  - ORB (Oriented FAST and Rotated
    BRIEF)

- o AKAZE (Accelerated-KAZE)[1]
- Process:
  - o Keypoints are detected in the image.
  - o Descriptors are computed for each keypoint, representing the local image information.
  - o Descriptors are matched between images to identify corresponding features.
- Advantages:
  - o Invariant to scale, rotation, and illumination changes (to varying degrees).
  - o Can be used for a wide range of object detection tasks.
- Disadvantages:
  - o Computationally more expensive than Haar cascades.
  - o May not be suitable for real-time applications with limited resources.

6.3 Tracking Objects Using Kalman Filters and Particle Filters

Kalman filters and particle filters are probabilistic methods for tracking objects over time, providing robust and accurate tracking results.

Kalman Filters:

- Concept: A Kalman filter is a recursive algorithm that estimates the state of a dynamic system from noisy measurements.
- Process:
    - The filter predicts the next state of the object based on its previous state and motion model.
    - The filter updates the state estimate based on the current measurement.
    - The filter provides an optimal estimate of the object's state, minimizing the estimation error.
- Advantages:

- Provides optimal state estimates for linear systems with Gaussian noise.
- Efficient and computationally inexpensive.
- Disadvantages:
  - Assumes a linear system and Gaussian noise, which may not always be accurate.
  - Can be sensitive to model inaccuracies.

Particle Filters:

- Concept: A particle filter is a recursive algorithm that approximates the probability distribution of an object's state using a set of particles.
- Process:
  - A set of particles is initialized, representing possible states of the object.
  - The particles are propagated according to a motion model.

- The particles are weighted based on the likelihood of the measurements.
- The state estimate is computed as the weighted average of the particles.
- Advantages:
  - Can handle nonlinear systems and non-Gaussian noise.
  - Robust to model inaccuracies and outliers.
- Disadvantages:
  - Computationally more expensive than Kalman filters.
  - Requires a large number of particles for accurate estimation.

OpenCV Implementation:

- cv::KalmanFilter: Class for implementing Kalman filters.
- No direct particle filter implementation in core OpenCV, but OpenCV provides the random number generation and matrix

manipulation tools needed to implement one.

These object detection and tracking techniques are essential for enabling robots to perceive and interact with dynamic environments. By mastering these skills, robotics developers can create robust and reliable perception systems for various applications.

Part III: Robotics Development with ROS

Chapter 7. Introduction to ROS and Robotics Development

This chapter introduces the Robot Operating System (ROS), a widely used framework for robotics software development. We will explore its key features, discuss fundamental concepts of robotics development, and provide a guide for setting up ROS with C++.

7.1 Overview of ROS and its Features

ROS is not an operating system in the traditional sense, but rather a meta-operating system or a framework that provides a collection of tools, libraries, and conventions for building complex robotic systems. It simplifies the development process by providing a standardized communication infrastructure and a rich ecosystem of pre-built packages.

Key Features of ROS:

- Distributed Computing: ROS enables distributed communication between different software components (nodes) running on the same or different computers.
- Message Passing: Nodes communicate by publishing and subscribing to messages, which are data structures that carry information.
- Service Calls: Nodes can provide services that other nodes can call, enabling request-response communication.
- Parameter Server: A centralized repository for storing and retrieving configuration parameters.
- Hardware Abstraction: ROS provides hardware abstraction layers, making it easier to interface with different sensors and actuators.
- Visualization Tools: ROS includes tools for visualizing robot data, such as RViz (3D visualization) and rqt (GUI framework).

- Simulation Tools: ROS integrates with simulation environments like Gazebo, allowing for testing and development in a virtual environment.
- Extensive Libraries: ROS provides a rich set of libraries for common robotics tasks, such as navigation, manipulation, and perception.
- Open Source: ROS is open-source, fostering a collaborative development community.
- Language Independence: While predominantly used with C++ and Python, ROS supports other languages as well.

Benefits of Using ROS for Robotics Development:

- Rapid Prototyping: ROS simplifies the development process, enabling faster prototyping and testing.
- Code Reusability: ROS promotes code reusability through its package-based architecture.

- Modularity: ROS encourages modular design, making it easier to develop and maintain complex robotic systems.
- Community Support: ROS has a large and active community, providing extensive support and resources.
- Integration with Existing Tools: ROS integrates with various existing tools and libraries, such as OpenCV and PCL.

7.2 Basic Concepts of Robotics Development

Robotics development involves a range of concepts and techniques, including perception, planning, control, and communication. ROS provides a framework for integrating these different aspects of robotics.

Key Concepts:

- Perception: The ability of a robot to sense and interpret its environment using sensors such as cameras, lidar, and sonar.
- Planning: The process of generating a sequence of actions that a robot can take

to achieve a goal, such as path planning and motion planning.

- Control: The process of executing the planned actions and controlling the robot's actuators to achieve the desired behavior.
- Localization: The ability of a robot to determine its position and orientation in its environment.
- Mapping: The process of creating a representation of the robot's environment.
- Navigation: The ability of a robot to move autonomously from one location to another.
- Manipulation: The ability of a robot to interact with objects in its environment.
- Communication: The ability of a robot to communicate with other robots or humans.
- Nodes: Executable processes in ROS that perform specific tasks.
- Topics: Named buses over which nodes exchange messages.
- Messages: Data structures that are published and subscribed to by nodes.

- Services: Request-response communication between nodes.
- Parameters: Configuration values that can be accessed and modified by nodes.
- Actionlib: a standardized interface for long-running tasks.

7.3 Setting up ROS with C++

To begin developing robotics applications with ROS and C++, you need to install ROS and configure your development environment.

Steps to Set up ROS with C++:

1. Install ROS:
   - Follow the official ROS installation instructions for your operating system (Ubuntu is the most common platform).
   - Choose the appropriate ROS distribution (e.g., Noetic, Humble, Iron).
   - Example for Ubuntu:
   - Bash

sudo apt update

sudo apt install curl gnupg lsb-release

sudo curl -sSL 'http://packages.ros.org/ros2/ubuntu/gpgkey.asc' | sudo gpg --dearmor -o /usr/share/keyrings/ros-archive-keyring.gpg

echo 'deb [arch=$(dpkg --print-architecture) signed-by=/usr/share/keyrings/ros-archive-keyring.gpg] http://packages.ros.org/ros2/ubuntu $(lsb_release -cs) main' | sudo tee /etc/apt/sources.list.d/ros2.list > /dev/null

sudo apt update

sudo apt install ros-humble-desktop # Replace 'humble' with your ROS distribution

- ○
- ○
- ○ Source the ROS setup file: source /opt/ros/humble/setup.bash

2. Create a ROS Workspace:
   - ○ Create a directory for your ROS workspace: mkdir -p ~/ros2_ws/src
   - ○ Navigate to the src directory: cd ~/ros2_ws/src

3. Create a ROS Package:

- Use the ros2 pkg create command to create a new ROS package.
- Example: ros2 pkg create my_package --build-type ament_cmake --dependencies rclcpp std_msgs

4. Write C++ Code:
   - Create a C++ source file in the src directory of your package.
   - Use the ROS C++ client library (rclcpp) to create nodes, publish and subscribe to topics, and call services.

5. Configure CMakeLists.txt:
   - Modify the CMakeLists.txt file in your package to specify the source files, dependencies, and build targets.

6. Build the Package:
   - Navigate to the root of your ROS workspace: cd ~/ros2_ws
   - Build the package using colcon build.

7. Source the Workspace:

- Source the workspace setup file: source install/setup.bash
8. Run the Node:
   - Use the ros2 run command to run your node.
   - Example: ros2 run my_package my_node

By following these steps, you can set up a ROS development environment and begin creating robotics applications with C++. ROS provides a powerful and flexible framework for building complex robotic systems, and mastering its concepts and tools is essential for robotics developers.

Chapter 8. ROS Nodes, Topics, and Services

This chapter delves into the core communication mechanisms of the Robot Operating System (ROS): nodes, topics, and services. We will explore how to create and manage ROS nodes, understand the concept of topics and messages, and utilize services for request-response communication.

8.1 Creating and Managing ROS Nodes

ROS nodes are the fundamental building blocks of a ROS system. They are executable processes that perform specific tasks, such as sensor data processing, motor control, or path planning.

Creating ROS Nodes:

- C++ Node Structure:

- A ROS node in C++ typically uses the rclcpp library.
- The node is created using the rclcpp::Node class.
- The main() function initializes the ROS communication system and creates the node.
- Example:
- C++

```cpp
#include "rclcpp/rclcpp.hpp"

int main(int argc, char * argv[]) {
    rclcpp::init(argc, argv);
    auto node = std::make_shared<rclcpp::Node>("my_node");
    RCLCPP_INFO(node->get_logger(), "My node has been started.");
    rclcpp::spin(node);
    rclcpp::shutdown();
    return 0;
}
```

-

o

- Node Management:
  - o rclcpp::init(): Initializes the ROS communication system.
  - o rclcpp::shutdown(): Terminates the ROS communication system.
  - o rclcpp::spin(): Blocks the node from exiting, allowing it to process incoming messages and service requests.
  - o rclcpp::Node::get_logger(): Used for logging information, warnings, and errors.
  - o RCLCPP_INFO(): A macro for logging informational messages.

8.2 Understanding ROS Topics and Messages

ROS topics are named buses over which nodes exchange messages. Messages are data structures that carry information. This publish-subscribe mechanism enables asynchronous communication between nodes.

ROS Topics:

- Publish-Subscribe Model: Nodes can publish messages to a topic or subscribe to a topic to receive messages.
- Asynchronous Communication: Nodes do not need to know the specific publishers or subscribers of a topic.
- Data Flow: Topics facilitate the flow of data between different parts of a robotic system.
- Example of publishing and subscribing to a topic.
  - Publisher:
  - C++

```cpp
#include "rclcpp/rclcpp.hpp"
#include "std_msgs/msg/string.hpp"

int main(int argc, char * argv[]) {
  rclcpp::init(argc, argv);
```

```cpp
                auto      node      =
std::make_shared<rclcpp::Node>("my_publisher
");
                auto      publisher      =
node->create_publisher<std_msgs::msg::String>
("my_topic", 10);
    auto message = std_msgs::msg::String();
    message.data = "Hello, ROS!";
    publisher->publish(message);
    rclcpp::shutdown();
    return 0;
}
```

-
-
- **Subscriber:**
- C++

```cpp
#include "rclcpp/rclcpp.hpp"
#include "std_msgs/msg/string.hpp"

void                          topic_callback(const
std_msgs::msg::String::SharedPtr msg) {
```

```
RCLCPP_INFO(rclcpp::get_logger("my_subscri
ber"), "Received: '%s'", msg->data.c_str());
}

int main(int argc, char * argv[]) {
    rclcpp::init(argc, argv);
                    auto        node      =
std::make_shared<rclcpp::Node>("my_subscribe
r");
                    auto    subscriber    =
node->create_subscription<std_msgs::msg::Strin
g>("my_topic", 10, topic_callback);
    rclcpp::spin(node);
    rclcpp::shutdown();
    return 0;
}
                o
                o
```

ROS Messages:

- Data Structures: Messages define the data that is exchanged between nodes.

- Message Definitions: Messages are defined in .msg files, which specify the data types and names of the fields.
- Standard Messages: ROS provides a set of standard messages, such as std_msgs (e.g., String, Int32, Float64) and sensor_msgs (e.g., Image, LaserScan).
- Custom Messages: Developers can create custom messages to suit the specific needs of their applications.

8.3 Using ROS Services for Communication

ROS services provide a request-response communication mechanism between nodes. This is useful for tasks that require a synchronous exchange of information.

ROS Services:

- Request-Response Communication: A client node sends a request to a server node, and the server node sends back a response.

- Service Definitions: Services are defined in .srv files, which specify the request and response data types.
- Service Server: A node that provides a service.
- Service Client: A node that calls a service.
- Example Service server and client.
  - Server:
  - C++

```cpp
#include "rclcpp/rclcpp.hpp"
#include "example_interfaces/srv/add_two_ints.hpp"

void                          add_two_ints(const
std::shared_ptr<example_interfaces::srv::AddTw
oInts::Request> request,

std::shared_ptr<example_interfaces::srv::AddTw
oInts::Response> response) {
  response->sum = request->a + request->b;

RCLCPP_INFO(rclcpp::get_logger("add_two_in
```

ts_server"), "Incoming request: a: %ld b: %ld", request->a, request->b);

RCLCPP_INFO(rclcpp::get_logger("add_two_in ts_server"), "sending back response: %ld", response->sum);
}

```
int main(int argc, char * argv[]) {
    rclcpp::init(argc, argv);
                        auto    node    =
std::make_shared<rclcpp::Node>("add_two_ints
_server");
                    auto    service    =
node->create_service<example_interfaces::srv::
AddTwoInts>("add_two_ints", add_two_ints);

RCLCPP_INFO(rclcpp::get_logger("add_two_in
ts_server"), "Ready to add two ints.");
    rclcpp::spin(node);
    rclcpp::shutdown();
    return 0;
}
```

○

- ○
  - ○ Client:
  - ○ C++

```cpp
#include "rclcpp/rclcpp.hpp"
#include "example_interfaces/srv/add_two_ints.hpp"

int main(int argc, char * argv[]) {
  rclcpp::init(argc, argv);
  auto node = std::make_shared<rclcpp::Node>("add_two_ints_client");
  auto client = node->create_client<example_interfaces::srv::AddTwoInts>("add_two_ints");
  auto request = std::make_shared<example_interfaces::srv::AddTwoInts::Request>();
  request->a = 2;
  request->b = 3;
```

```cpp
        auto result =
client->async_send_request(request);
    if (rclcpp::spin_until_future_complete(node,
result) ==
rclcpp::FutureReturnCode::SUCCESS) {

RCLCPP_INFO(rclcpp::get_logger("add_two_in
ts_client"), "Result: %ld", result.get()->sum);
    } else {

RCLCPP_ERROR(rclcpp::get_logger("add_two
_ints_client"), "Failed to call service
add_two_ints");
    }
    rclcpp::shutdown();
    return 0;
}
```

○

○

By mastering nodes, topics, and services, developers can build robust and flexible ROS systems for a wide range of robotics applications.

Chapter 9. ROS Navigation and Mapping

This chapter introduces the fundamental concepts of navigation and mapping in robotics using the Robot Operating System (ROS). We will explore the ROS navigation stack, mapping tools, and techniques for creating and managing maps, enabling robots to autonomously navigate and explore their environments.

9.1 Introduction to Navigation and Mapping

Navigation and mapping are essential capabilities for autonomous robots. Navigation enables robots to move from one location to another, while mapping allows robots to build representations of their environments.

Navigation:

- Goal: To enable a robot to move autonomously from a starting point to a goal location.
- Components:
    - Localization: Determining the robot's pose (position and orientation) in the environment.
    - Mapping: Creating a representation of the environment.
    - Path Planning: Generating a collision-free path from the robot's current pose to the goal pose.
    - Motion Control: Executing the planned path by controlling the robot's actuators.
- ROS Navigation Stack: A collection of ROS packages that provide navigation capabilities.

Mapping:

- Goal: To create a representation of the robot's environment.
- Types of Maps:

- Occupancy Grid Maps: Represent the environment as a grid, where each cell indicates whether it is occupied or free.
- Point Cloud Maps: Represent the environment as a collection of 3D points.
- Feature-Based Maps: Represent the environment using extracted features, such as corners and edges.
- Mapping Techniques:
  - SLAM (Simultaneous Localization and Mapping): Building a map while simultaneously localizing the robot.
  - Static Mapping: Creating a map of a static environment.

9.2 Using ROS Navigation and Mapping Tools

ROS provides a suite of tools and packages for navigation and mapping, simplifying the development of autonomous robots.

ROS Navigation Stack:

- move_base: The core navigation package, responsible for path planning and motion control.
- amcl (Adaptive Monte Carlo Localization): A probabilistic localization algorithm that estimates the robot's pose using a particle filter.
- gmapping: A SLAM package that creates occupancy grid maps using laser scan data.
- map_server: A package that loads and saves map data.
- costmap_2d: A package that provides costmaps for path planning, representing the cost of traversing different areas of the environment.
- navigation_msgs: ROS message definitions for navigation-related data.
- teb_local_planner and dwa_local_planner: packages that implement local path planners.

Mapping Tools:

- gmapping: A SLAM package that uses laser scan data to create occupancy grid maps.
- cartographer: A SLAM package developed by Google, known for its robustness and accuracy.
- hector_slam: A SLAM package that does not require odometry data, suitable for robots with poor odometry.
- map_saver: A tool for saving maps created by SLAM packages.
- map_server: A tool for loading and serving maps for navigation.
- RViz: A 3D visualization tool that can display maps, robot poses, and sensor data.

Example: Using gmapping and move_base:

1. Launch gmapping:
   - Launch the gmapping node, along with the necessary sensor drivers.
   - Example launch file:
   - XML

```xml
<launch>
    <node pkg="gmapping" type="slam_gmapping" name="slam_gmapping">
  <remap from="scan" to="scan"/>
        <param name="map_update_interval" value="5.0"/>
  <param name="xmin" value="-10.0"/>
  <param name="ymin" value="-10.0"/>
  <param name="xmax" value="10.0"/>
  <param name="ymax" value="10.0"/>
  <param name="delta" value="0.05"/>
 </node>
</launch>
```

- o
- o

2. Drive the Robot:
   - o Manually drive the robot around the environment to collect laser scan data.
3. Save the Map:
   - o Use the map_saver tool to save the generated map:
   - o Bash

rosrun map_server map_saver -f my_map

- ○
- ○

4. Launch move_base:
   - ○ Launch the move_base node, along with the necessary localization and planning nodes.
   - ○ Example launch file:
   - ○ XML

```xml
<launch>
  <node pkg="move_base" type="move_base" name="move_base" output="screen">
    <rosparam file="$(find my_robot_config)/costmap_common_params.yaml" command="load" ns="global_costmap" />
    <rosparam file="$(find my_robot_config)/costmap_common_params.yaml" command="load" ns="local_costmap" />
    <rosparam file="$(find my_robot_config)/local_costmap_params.yaml" command="load" ns="local_costmap" />
```

```
                    <rosparam        file="$(find
my_robot_config)/global_costmap_params.yaml
" command="load" ns="global_costmap" />
                    <rosparam        file="$(find
my_robot_config)/base_local_planner_params.y
aml" command="load" />
  </node>
  <node pkg="amcl" type="amcl" name="amcl">
                    <rosparam        file="$(find
my_robot_config)/amcl_params.yaml"
command="load" />
  </node>
  <node pkg="map_server" type="map_server"
name="map_server"              args="$(find
my_robot_config)/my_map.yaml"/>
</launch>
```

- o
- o

5. Send Navigation Goals:
   - o Use RViz or the rostopic pub command to send navigation goals to the move_base node.

9.3 Creating and Managing Maps

Creating and managing accurate maps is crucial for reliable robot navigation.

Creating Maps:

- SLAM: Use SLAM packages like gmapping, cartographer, or hector_slam to create maps in real-time.
- Static Mapping: Create maps offline using sensor data collected from a static environment.
- Map Editing: Use image editing software to modify maps, such as adding or removing obstacles.

Managing Maps:

- Map Storage: Store maps in a suitable format, such as .pgm (for image data) and .yaml (for map metadata).
- Map Loading: Use the map_server package to load maps for navigation.

- Map Updates: Update maps as the environment changes or as the robot explores new areas.
- Map Transformations: Apply transformations to maps, such as rotations and translations.

These ROS navigation and mapping tools provide a powerful and flexible framework for enabling robots to autonomously navigate and explore their environments. By mastering these techniques, robotics developers can create sophisticated navigation systems for various applications.

Part IV: Advanced Robotics Development

Chapter 10. Sensor Integration and Processing

This chapter explores the crucial aspect of sensor integration and processing in robotics, enabling robots to perceive and understand their environment. We will cover the fundamentals of sensor integration, the use of common sensors like GPS, IMU, and cameras, and techniques for processing sensor data using filters and algorithms.

10.1 Introduction to Sensor Integration and Processing

Sensor integration involves combining data from multiple sensors to create a more complete and accurate understanding of the robot's environment. Sensor processing involves filtering, transforming, and analyzing sensor data to extract relevant information.

Sensor Integration:

- Goal: To combine data from multiple sensors to improve accuracy, robustness, and redundancy.
- Techniques:
  - Sensor Fusion: Combining data from different sensor types to create a unified representation.
  - Data Association: Matching sensor measurements to objects or features in the environment.
  - Calibration: Adjusting sensor measurements to compensate for errors and biases.
- Benefits:
  - Improved accuracy and robustness.
  - Increased redundancy and fault tolerance.
  - Enhanced perception capabilities.

Sensor Processing:

- Goal: To extract relevant information from sensor data.
- Techniques:
    - Filtering: Removing noise and outliers from sensor data.
    - Transformation: Converting sensor data to a common coordinate frame.
    - Feature Extraction: Identifying relevant features in sensor data.
    - Data Analysis: Interpreting sensor data to understand the environment.
- Benefits:
    - Improved data quality.
    - Reduced computational load.
    - Enhanced understanding of the environment.

10.2 Using Sensors Such as GPS, IMU, and Cameras

Robots utilize a variety of sensors to perceive their surroundings. We will explore the use of common sensors like GPS, IMU, and cameras.

GPS (Global Positioning System):

- Purpose: Provides global position and velocity information.
- Data: Latitude, longitude, altitude, velocity, and time.
- Applications: Outdoor navigation, localization, and mapping.
- ROS Integration:
  - sensor_msgs/NavSatFix: ROS message for GPS data.
  - nmea_navsat_driver: ROS package for interfacing with GPS receivers.
- Considerations:
  - Limited accuracy in urban environments.
  - Susceptible to signal blockage and interference.

IMU (Inertial Measurement Unit):

- Purpose: Measures acceleration and angular velocity.
- Data: Acceleration (linear acceleration) and angular velocity (rotation rate).
- Applications: Orientation estimation, motion tracking, and stabilization.
- ROS Integration:
    - sensor_msgs/Imu: ROS message for IMU data.
    - imu_tools: ROS package for processing IMU data.
- Considerations:
    - Accumulation of drift over time.
    - Susceptible to noise and vibrations.

Cameras:

- Purpose: Captures images and videos of the environment.
- Data: Pixel intensity values representing color and brightness.
- Applications: Object detection, object tracking, visual navigation, and 3D reconstruction.

- ROS Integration:
    - sensor_msgs/Image: ROS message for image data.
    - sensor_msgs/CameraInfo: ROS message for camera calibration data.
    - usb_cam or realsense2_camera: ROS packages for interfacing with cameras.
- Considerations:
    - Computationally intensive processing.
    - Susceptible to lighting conditions and occlusion.

10.3 Processing Sensor Data Using Filters and Algorithms

Sensor data often contains noise and errors, requiring filtering and processing to extract meaningful information.

Filtering:

- Purpose: To remove noise and outliers from sensor data.
- Types of Filters:
    - Low-Pass Filters: Smooth out high-frequency noise.
    - High-Pass Filters: Emphasize high-frequency changes.
    - Kalman Filters: Estimate the state of a dynamic system from noisy measurements.
    - Particle Filters: Approximate the probability distribution of a system's state.
    - Median Filters: Remove outliers by replacing values with the median.
- Applications:
    - Smoothing sensor readings.
    - Removing noise from images.
    - Estimating robot pose.

Algorithms:

- Purpose: To extract relevant information from sensor data.

- Types of Algorithms:
  - Feature Detection and Matching: Identify and match features in images.
  - Object Detection and Tracking: Identify and track objects in images and videos.
  - Odometry Estimation: Estimate robot motion from wheel encoder data.
  - SLAM (Simultaneous Localization and Mapping): Build a map while simultaneously localizing the robot.
- Applications:
  - Object recognition.
  - Robot navigation.
  - Map building.

Example: Filtering IMU data using a Kalman Filter:

C++

```
#include <rclcpp/rclcpp.hpp>
```

```cpp
#include <sensor_msgs/msg/imu.hpp>
#include <opencv2/core.hpp>
#include <opencv2/video/tracking.hpp>

class ImuFilter : public rclcpp::Node {
public:
  ImuFilter() : Node("imu_filter") {
                    subscription_ =
this->create_subscription<sensor_msgs::msg::Imu>(
                    "imu/data_raw",  10,
std::bind(&ImuFilter::imuCallback,          this,
std::placeholders::_1));

          kalmanFilter_.init(6, 3, 0); // 6 state
variables, 3 measurement variables
          kalmanFilter_.transitionMatrix =
(cv::Mat_<float>(6, 6) << 1, 0, 0, 1, 0, 0,
                                0, 1, 0,
0, 1, 0,
                                0, 0, 1,
0, 0, 1,
                                0, 0, 0,
1, 0, 0,
```

```
                                    0, 0, 0,
0, 1, 0,
                                    0, 0, 0,
0, 0, 1);
        kalmanFilter_.measurementMatrix =
(cv::Mat_<float>(3, 6) << 1, 0, 0, 0, 0, 0,
                                    0, 1,
0, 0, 0, 0,
                                    0, 0,
1, 0, 0, 0);

cv::setIdentity(kalmanFilter_.processNoiseCov,
cv::Scalar::all(1e-5));

cv::setIdentity(kalmanFilter_.measurementNoise
Cov, cv::Scalar::all(1e-1));
    cv::setIdentity(kalmanFilter_.errorCovPost,
cv::Scalar::all(1));
  }

private:
                void    imuCallback(const
sensor_msgs::msg::Imu::SharedPtr msg) {
```

```cpp
        cv::Mat    measurement    =
(cv::Mat_<float>(3,            1)            <<
msg->angular_velocity.x,

msg->angular_velocity.y,

msg->angular_velocity.z);

            cv::Mat    prediction    =
kalmanFilter_.predict();
            cv::Mat    corrected    =
kalmanFilter_.correct(measurement);

        RCLCPP_INFO(this->get_logger(),
"Filtered angular velocity: x=%f, y=%f, z=%f",
                corrected.at<float>(0),
corrected.at<float>(1), corrected.at<float>(2));
  }


rclcpp::Subscription<sensor_msgs::msg::Imu>::
SharedPtr subscription_;
  cv::KalmanFilter kalmanFilter_;
};
```

```cpp
int main(int argc, char * argv[]) {
    rclcpp::init(argc, argv);
    rclcpp::spin(std::make_shared<ImuFilter>());
    rclcpp::shutdown();
    return 0;
}
```

This chapter provides a foundation for integrating and processing sensor data in robotics applications. By mastering these techniques, robotics developers can create robust and reliable perception systems for various applications.

Chapter 11. Motion Planning and Control

This chapter delves into the critical aspects of motion planning and control, which enable robots to autonomously navigate and manipulate objects in their environment. We will explore motion planning algorithms like A* and D*, and control techniques such as PID controllers and Model Predictive Control (MPC).

11.1 Introduction to Motion Planning and Control

Motion planning and control are essential for enabling robots to execute desired tasks in a safe and efficient manner.

Motion Planning:

- Goal: To generate a feasible and optimal path for a robot to move from a starting point to a goal point, while avoiding obstacles and respecting constraints.

- Types of Planning:
  - Global Planning: Generating a path for the entire workspace.
  - Local Planning: Generating a path for a local region around the robot.
- Key Considerations:
  - Obstacle Avoidance: Ensuring the robot does not collide with obstacles.
  - Path Optimality: Finding the shortest or most efficient path.
  - Kinematic and Dynamic Constraints: Respecting the robot's physical limitations.
  - Computational Efficiency: Generating paths in real-time.

Motion Control:

- Goal: To execute the planned path by controlling the robot's actuators.
- Types of Control:

- Open-Loop Control: Executing commands without feedback.
- Closed-Loop Control: Using feedback to correct errors and maintain desired behavior.
- Key Considerations:
  - Stability: Ensuring the robot's motion is stable and does not oscillate.
  - Accuracy: Minimizing errors between the desired and actual motion.
  - Robustness: Maintaining performance in the presence of disturbances.
  - Real-time Performance: Executing control commands in real-time.

11.2 Using Motion Planning Algorithms Such as A and D**

Motion planning algorithms are used to generate paths for robots in complex environments.

*A (A-Star) Algorithm:**

- Concept: A* is a graph search algorithm that finds the shortest path between two points in a graph or grid.
- Process:
  - A* uses a heuristic function to estimate the cost of reaching the goal from any given node.
  - A* explores the graph by expanding nodes with the lowest estimated total cost.
  - A* guarantees to find the optimal path if the heuristic function is admissible (never overestimates the cost).
- Applications:
  - Path planning in grid-based environments.
  - Navigation in static environments.
- Advantages:
  - Guarantees to find the optimal path.
  - Efficient for many path planning problems.
- Disadvantages:

- Memory-intensive for large graphs.
- Not suitable for dynamic environments.

D (Dynamic A-Star) Algorithm:

- Concept: D* is an incremental search algorithm that efficiently replans paths in dynamic or partially known environments.
- Process:
  - D* maintains a search tree and updates it incrementally as the environment changes.
  - D* can quickly replan paths by reusing information from previous searches.
- Applications:
  - Path planning in dynamic environments.
  - Navigation in partially known environments.
- Advantages:
  - Efficient for replanning in dynamic environments.

- Can handle changes in the environment.
- Disadvantages:
  - More complex than A*.
  - Can be computationally expensive for large changes.

11.3 Controlling Robots Using PID Controllers and Model Predictive Control

Control techniques are used to execute the planned paths by controlling the robot's actuators.

PID (Proportional-Integral-Derivative) Controllers:

- Concept: PID controllers are widely used feedback control algorithms that adjust the control output based on the error between the desired and actual values.
- Process:
  - The proportional term adjusts the output based on the current error.

- The integral term eliminates steady-state errors.
  - The derivative term anticipates future errors.
- Applications:
  - Motor control.
  - Position control.
  - Velocity control.
- Advantages:
  - Simple to implement and tune.
  - Effective for many control problems.
- Disadvantages:
  - Can be difficult to tune for complex systems.
  - May not be optimal for nonlinear systems.

Model Predictive Control (MPC):

- Concept: MPC is an advanced control technique that uses a model of the system to predict future behavior and optimize control actions[1] over a finite time horizon.

- Process:
  - MPC uses a model of the system to predict future states.
  - MPC optimizes control actions to minimize a cost function that considers desired behavior and constraints.
  - MPC applies the first control action and repeats the optimization at each time step.
- Applications:
  - Robotic manipulation.
  - Autonomous driving.
  - Trajectory tracking.
- Advantages:
  - Can handle complex systems and constraints.
  - Provides optimal control actions.
- Disadvantages:
  - Computationally expensive.
  - Requires an accurate model of the system.

Example: PID Control in ROS:

C++

```cpp
#include <rclcpp/rclcpp.hpp>
#include <geometry_msgs/msg/twist.hpp>

class PidController : public rclcpp::Node {
public:
  PidController() : Node("pid_controller") {
    publisher_ =
this->create_publisher<geometry_msgs::msg::T
wist>("cmd_vel", 10);
    timer_ =
this->create_wall_timer(std::chrono::millisecond
s(100),    std::bind(&PidController::controlLoop,
this));
    desired_velocity_ = 1.0;
    current_velocity_ = 0.0;
    error_ = 0.0;
    integral_ = 0.0;
    previous_error_ = 0.0;
    kp_ = 1.0;
    ki_ = 0.1;
    kd_ = 0.01;
```

```cpp
  }

private:
  void controlLoop() {
    error_ = desired_velocity_ - current_velocity_;
    integral_ += error_;
    double derivative_ = error_ - previous_error_;
    double output_ = kp_ * error_ + ki_ * integral_ + kd_ * derivative_;
    geometry_msgs::msg::Twist twist;
    twist.linear.x = output_;
    publisher_->publish(twist);
    previous_error_ = error_;
    current_velocity_ += output_ * 0.1; // Simulated velocity update
  }


  rclcpp::Publisher<geometry_msgs::msg::Twist>::SharedPtr publisher_;
  rclcpp::TimerBase::SharedPtr timer_;
  double desired_velocity_;
```

```cpp
    double current_velocity_;
    double error_;
    double integral_;
    double previous_error_;
    double kp_;
    double ki_;
    double kd_;
};

int main(int argc, char * argv[]) {
    rclcpp::init(argc, argv);

rclcpp::spin(std::make_shared<PidController>())
;
    rclcpp::shutdown();
    return 0;
}
```

This chapter provides an overview of motion planning and control techniques, enabling robots to navigate and manipulate objects effectively. By mastering these skills, robotics developers can create sophisticated and autonomous robots.

Chapter 12. Human-Robot Interaction and Interface Design

This chapter explores the critical aspects of human-robot interaction (HRI) and interface design, which are essential for creating robots that can effectively communicate and collaborate with humans. We will cover the fundamentals of HRI, designing user interfaces for robots, and utilizing speech recognition and synthesis for seamless communication.

12.1 Introduction to Human-Robot Interaction and Interface Design

Human-robot interaction (HRI) is a multidisciplinary field that studies the interaction between humans and robots. Effective HRI is crucial for creating robots that are safe, intuitive, and beneficial to humans. Interface design plays a vital role in facilitating this interaction.

Human-Robot Interaction (HRI):

- Goal: To create robots that can effectively communicate, collaborate, and coexist with humans.
- Key Considerations:
  - Safety: Ensuring the robot's actions do not pose a threat to humans.
  - Usability: Designing interfaces that are easy to understand and use.
  - Social Acceptability: Creating robots that are perceived as friendly and approachable.
  - Communication: Enabling robots to convey information and understand human intent.
  - Collaboration: Designing robots that can work alongside humans to achieve shared goals.
- HRI Modalities:
  - Visual Communication: Using displays, gestures, and facial expressions.
  - Auditory Communication: Using speech, sounds, and tones.

- Tactile Communication: Using touch and haptic feedback.
- Kinesthetic Communication: Using physical interaction and movement.

Interface Design for Robotics:

- Goal: To create user interfaces that are intuitive, efficient, and appropriate for the target users and applications.
- Key Principles:
  - User-Centered Design: Focusing on the needs and preferences of the users.
  - Simplicity and Clarity: Avoiding complex or ambiguous interfaces.
  - Feedback and Confirmation: Providing clear feedback on user actions.
  - Error Prevention and Recovery: Designing interfaces that minimize errors and provide recovery mechanisms.

- Context Awareness: Adapting the interface to the user's context and environment.

12.2 Designing User Interfaces for Robots

Designing effective user interfaces for robots requires careful consideration of the robot's capabilities, the user's needs, and the application's context.

Types of Robot User Interfaces:

- Graphical User Interfaces (GUIs): Using displays and touchscreens to interact with the robot.
- Voice User Interfaces (VUIs): Using speech recognition and synthesis to communicate with the robot.
- Gesture-Based Interfaces: Using hand gestures and body movements to control the robot.
- Haptic Interfaces: Using touch and force feedback to interact with the robot.

- Augmented Reality (AR) Interfaces: Overlaying virtual information onto the real world to enhance interaction.

Design Considerations:

- Robot Mobility and Autonomy: Designing interfaces that are suitable for mobile and autonomous robots.
- User Expertise and Experience: Adapting interfaces to the user's level of expertise.
- Task Complexity and Frequency: Designing interfaces that are efficient for frequent and complex tasks.
- Environmental Factors: Considering the user's environment, such as lighting, noise, and space.
- Robot Embodiment and Appearance: Designing interfaces that are consistent with the robot's physical appearance.

12.3 Using Speech Recognition and Synthesis for Human-Robot Interaction

Speech recognition and synthesis are powerful tools for enabling natural and intuitive communication between humans and robots.

Speech Recognition:

- Goal: To convert human speech into text or commands that the robot can understand.
- Techniques:
    - Hidden Markov Models (HMMs): Statistical models that represent the probabilistic relationships between speech sounds.
    - Deep Learning: Neural networks that learn to recognize speech patterns.
    - Cloud-Based Speech Recognition: Using online services to process speech data.
- ROS Integration:
    - pocketsphinx: An open-source speech recognition library.
    - google_speech: ROS package for using Google Cloud Speech API.

- vosk: A lightweight offline speech recognition engine.

Speech Synthesis:

- Goal: To convert text or commands into human-like speech that the robot can produce.
- Techniques:
  - Concatenative Synthesis: Combining recorded speech fragments to create new speech.
  - Parametric Synthesis: Generating speech from acoustic parameters.
  - Deep Learning: Neural networks that learn to generate speech.
- ROS Integration:
  - festival: An open-source speech synthesis system.
  - espeak_tts: A software speech synthesizer that speaks English and other languages.
  - gtts: A package that uses Google Text-to-Speech API.

Example: Simple Speech Interaction in ROS:

C++

```cpp
#include <rclcpp/rclcpp.hpp>
#include <std_msgs/msg/string.hpp>
#include <iostream>

class SpeechInteraction : public rclcpp::Node {
public:
    SpeechInteraction() : Node("speech_interaction") {
        speech_publisher_ = this->create_publisher<std_msgs::msg::String>(
            "speech_output", 10);
        command_subscriber_ = this->create_subscription<std_msgs::msg::String>("speech_input", 10,
            std::bind(&SpeechInteraction::commandCallback, this, std::placeholders::_1));
    }

private:
    void commandCallback(const std_msgs::msg::String::SharedPtr msg) {
```

```cpp
    std::string command = msg->data;
    if (command == "hello") {
      publishSpeech("Hello, human!");
    } else if (command == "goodbye") {
      publishSpeech("Goodbye!");
    } else {
        publishSpeech("I don't understand that
command.");
    }
  }

  void publishSpeech(const std::string& text) {
    std_msgs::msg::String speech_msg;
    speech_msg.data = text;
    speech_publisher_->publish(speech_msg);
  }


rclcpp::Publisher<std_msgs::msg::String>::Shar
edPtr speech_publisher_;

rclcpp::Subscription<std_msgs::msg::String>::S
haredPtr command_subscriber_;
};
```

```cpp
int main(int argc, char * argv[]) {
    rclcpp::init(argc, argv);

rclcpp::spin(std::make_shared<SpeechInteractio
n>());
    rclcpp::shutdown();
    return 0;
}
```

This chapter provides an overview of human-robot interaction and interface design, enabling the creation of robots that can effectively communicate and collaborate with humans.

By mastering these skills, robotics developers can create sophisticated and user-friendly robotic systems.

Part V: Case Studies and Projects

Chapter 13. Case Study: Autonomous Robot Navigation

This chapter presents a comprehensive case study on autonomous robot navigation, demonstrating the practical application of ROS and OpenCV for building a functional navigation system. We will cover the overview of autonomous navigation, and the implementation details using ROS and OpenCV.

13.1 Overview of Autonomous Robot Navigation

Autonomous robot navigation involves enabling a robot to move from one location to another without human intervention. This requires a combination of perception, planning, and control capabilities.

Key Components of Autonomous Navigation:

- Localization:
  - Determining the robot's pose (position and orientation) in its environment.
  - Techniques:
    - Odometry (wheel encoders, IMU).
    - SLAM (Simultaneous Localization and Mapping).
    - Sensor fusion (GPS, lidar, cameras).
- Mapping:
  - Creating a representation of the robot's environment.
  - Types of maps:
    - Occupancy grid maps.
    - Point cloud maps.
    - Feature-based maps.
  - Mapping techniques:
    - SLAM (Gmapping, Cartographer).
    - Static mapping.
- Path Planning:

- o Generating a collision-free path from the robot's current pose to the goal pose.
- o Algorithms:
  - A*.
  - D*.
  - RRT (Rapidly-exploring Random Tree).
  - TEB (Timed-Elastic-Band).
  - DWA (Dynamic Window Approach).
- Motion Control:
  - o Executing the planned path by controlling the robot's actuators.
  - o Techniques:
    - PID controllers.
    - Model Predictive Control (MPC).
    - Velocity control.
    - Trajectory following.
- Perception:
  - o Using sensors like Cameras, Lidar, and Sonar to understand the environment.

o Object detection, Obstacle avoidance, and environmental awareness.

13.2 Implementing Autonomous Navigation Using ROS and OpenCV

This section outlines the steps involved in implementing an autonomous navigation system using ROS and OpenCV.

1. System Architecture:

- Sensors:
  o Lidar (for obstacle detection and mapping).
  o Camera (for object recognition and visual navigation).
  o Odometry (for pose estimation).
- ROS Nodes:
  o Sensor Drivers: Nodes that interface with the robot's sensors.
  o Mapping Node: A node that builds a map of the environment (e.g., using gmapping or cartographer).

- Localization Node: A node that estimates the robot's pose (e.g., using amcl).
- Path Planning Node: A node that generates a path to the goal (e.g., using move_base).
- Motion Control Node: A node that controls the robot's actuators to follow the planned path.
- Perception node: A node that processes camera data for object and obstacle recognition.
- OpenCV integration:
  - Used in the perception node for image processing.
  - Used for tasks like object detection, feature matching, and obstacle avoidance.

2. Implementation Steps:

- Sensor Integration:
  - Install and configure ROS drivers for the robot's sensors.

- Publish sensor data as ROS messages.
- Mapping:
  - Launch a SLAM node (e.g., gmapping) to build a map of the environment.
  - Drive the robot around the environment to collect sensor data.
  - Save the generated map using map_saver.
- Localization:
  - Launch the amcl node to estimate the robot's pose.
  - Load the saved map using map_server.
  - Configure amcl parameters for accurate localization.
- Path Planning:
  - Launch the move_base node to generate and execute paths.
  - Configure move_base parameters for path planning and motion control.

- o Use RViz or the rostopic pub command to send navigation goals.
- Motion Control:
  - o Configure the motion control node to control the robot's actuators based on the planned path.
  - o Use PID controllers or other control algorithms to achieve accurate motion.
- Perception:
  - o Integrate OpenCV into a ROS node.
  - o Use OpenCV to process camera data.
  - o Implement object detection using Haar cascades, or deep learning models.
  - o Implement obstacle avoidance using image processing techniques.
- Testing and Tuning:
  - o Test the navigation system in a simulated or real environment.
  - o Tune the parameters of the localization, path planning, and motion control nodes.

- Evaluate the performance of the navigation system.

3. Example ROS Launch File (Simplified):

XML

```
<launch>
  <node pkg="map_server" type="map_server" name="map_server" args="$(find my_map_package)/my_map.yaml"/>

  <node pkg="amcl" type="amcl" name="amcl" output="screen">
    <rosparam file="$(find my_robot_config)/amcl_params.yaml" command="load" />
  </node>

  <node pkg="move_base" type="move_base" namc="move_base" output="screen">
    <rosparam file="$(find my_robot_config)/costmap_common_params.yaml" command="load" ns="global_costmap" />
```

```xml
            <rosparam        file="$(find
my_robot_config)/costmap_common_params.ya
ml" command="load" ns="local_costmap" />
            <rosparam        file="$(find
my_robot_config)/local_costmap_params.yaml"
command="load" ns="local_costmap" />
            <rosparam        file="$(find
my_robot_config)/global_costmap_params.yaml
" command="load" ns="global_costmap" />
            <rosparam        file="$(find
my_robot_config)/base_local_planner_params.y
aml" command="load" />
  </node>

   <node pkg="lidar_driver" type="lidar_node"
name="lidar_node"/>


            <node        pkg="camera_driver"
type="camera_node" name="camera_node"/>
            <node        pkg="perception"
type="perception_node"
name="perception_node"/>

</launch>
```

This case study demonstrates the practical application of ROS and OpenCV for building an autonomous robot navigation system. By following these steps and adapting them to specific robot platforms and environments, robotics developers can create robust and reliable navigation systems.

Chapter 14. Case Study: Object Recognition and Manipulation

This chapter presents a comprehensive case study on object recognition and manipulation, demonstrating the practical application of ROS and OpenCV for building a functional robotic manipulation system. We will cover the overview of object recognition and manipulation, and the implementation details using ROS and OpenCV.

14.1 Overview of Object Recognition and Manipulation

Object recognition and manipulation are fundamental capabilities for robots that interact with their environment. Object recognition involves identifying and locating objects, while manipulation involves grasping, moving, and placing objects.

Object Recognition:

- Goal: To identify and locate objects of interest in the robot's environment.
- Techniques:
    - Image processing (OpenCV).
    - Feature detection and matching (SIFT, SURF, ORB).
    - Object detection (Haar cascades, deep learning models).
    - 3D object recognition (point cloud processing).
- Key Considerations:
    - Robustness to variations in lighting, scale, and orientation.
    - Real-time performance.
    - Accuracy and reliability.

Object Manipulation:

- Goal: To enable a robot to grasp, move, and place objects.
- Components:
    - Robotic arm and end-effector.
    - Grasping planning.

- Motion planning.
- Force control.
- Key Considerations:
  - Grasp stability and reliability.
  - Collision avoidance.
  - Precision and accuracy.
  - Force control for delicate objects.

14.2 Implementing Object Recognition and Manipulation Using ROS and OpenCV

This section outlines the steps involved in implementing an object recognition and manipulation system using ROS and OpenCV.

1. System Architecture:

- Sensors:
  - Camera (for object recognition).
  - Depth sensor (for 3D object localization).
  - Force/torque sensor (for force control).
- Robotic Arm and End-Effector:

- A robotic arm with multiple degrees of freedom.
- An end-effector (gripper) for grasping objects.
- ROS Nodes:
  - Camera Driver: A node that interfaces with the camera.
  - Object Recognition Node: A node that processes camera data and identifies objects.
  - 3D Localization Node: A node that uses depth data to determine the 3D pose of objects.
  - Grasping Planning Node: A node that generates grasp poses.
  - Motion Planning Node: A node that generates collision-free trajectories for the robotic arm.
  - Arm Control Node: A node that controls the robotic arm's movements.
  - Force Control Node: a node that uses force sensor data to control the grasping force.

- OpenCV Integration:
  - Used in the object recognition node for image processing.
  - Used for tasks like object detection, feature matching, and pose estimation.

2. Implementation Steps:

- Sensor Integration:
  - Install and configure ROS drivers for the camera and depth sensor.
  - Publish sensor data as ROS messages.
- Object Recognition:
  - Use OpenCV to process camera images.
  - Implement object detection using deep learning models (e.g., YOLO, SSD) or feature-based methods (e.g., ORB).
  - Determine the 2D pose of the detected objects.
- 3D Localization:

- o Use depth data to determine the 3D pose of the detected objects.
- o Transform the object's pose from camera coordinates to robot base coordinates.
- Grasping Planning:
  - o Generate grasp poses based on the object's 3D pose and shape.
  - o Consider grasp stability and accessibility.
- Motion Planning:
  - o Use motion planning algorithms (e.g., MoveIt!) to generate collision-free trajectories for the robotic arm.
  - o Plan the arm's movement to reach the grasp pose.
- Arm Control:
  - o Control the robotic arm's actuators to follow the planned trajectory.
  - o Use ROS control packages to interface with the arm's controllers.
- Force Control:
  - o Integrate force/torque sensor data.

- Implement a force control loop to regulate the grasping force.
- Prevent damage to delicate objects.
- Testing and Tuning:
  - Test the object recognition and manipulation system in a simulated or real environment.
  - Tune the parameters of the object recognition, grasping planning, and motion control nodes.
  - Evaluate the performance of the system in terms of accuracy, reliability, and speed.

3. Example ROS Nodes and Integration:

- Object Recognition Node (using OpenCV and YOLO):
  - Subscribes to camera image topics.
  - Uses OpenCV's DNN module to run YOLO object detection.
  - Publishes detected object poses as ROS messages.
- 3D Localization Node (using depth data):

- Subscribes to depth image topics.
- Uses point cloud processing techniques to determine object 3D poses.
- Publishes object 3D poses as ROS messages.

- Grasping Planning Node:
  - Subscribes to object 3D pose topics.
  - Generates grasp poses based on object shape and pose.
  - Publishes grasp poses as ROS messages.

- Motion Planning Node (using MoveIt!):
  - Receives grasp poses as input.
  - Generates collision-free trajectories for the robotic arm.
  - Sends arm control commands to the arm control node.

- Arm Control Node:
  - Receives arm control commands.
  - Interfaces with the robotic arm's controllers.
  - Executes the arm's movements.

This case study demonstrates the practical application of ROS and OpenCV for building an object recognition and manipulation system. By following these steps and adapting them to specific robot platforms and environments, robotics developers can create sophisticated and functional manipulation systems.

Chapter 15. Case Study: Human-Robot Interaction and Collaboration

This chapter presents a comprehensive case study on human-robot interaction (HRI) and collaboration, demonstrating the practical application of ROS and OpenCV for building a system that enables seamless interaction and collaborative tasks between humans and robots. We will cover the overview of HRI and collaboration, and the implementation details using ROS and OpenCV.

15.1 Overview of Human-Robot Interaction and Collaboration

Human-robot interaction (HRI) focuses on designing robots that can effectively communicate and collaborate with humans. Collaboration extends HRI by enabling robots and humans to work together to achieve shared goals.

Human-Robot Interaction (HRI):

- Goal: To create robots that can effectively communicate and interact with humans in a natural and intuitive way.
- Key Aspects:
    - Communication: Enabling robots to understand and respond to human commands.
    - Social Interaction: Designing robots that can engage in social interactions.
    - Safety: Ensuring the robot's actions do not pose a threat to humans.
    - Usability: Designing interfaces that are easy to understand and use.
- HRI Modalities:
    - Speech Recognition and Synthesis: Using voice commands and responses.
    - Gesture Recognition: Interpreting hand gestures and body movements.

- Facial Expression Recognition: Understanding human emotions.
- Visual Communication: Using displays and visual cues.
- Haptic Feedback: Providing tactile feedback to humans.

Human-Robot Collaboration:

- Goal: To enable robots and humans to work together to achieve shared goals.
- Key Aspects:
  - Shared Understanding: Ensuring both the robot and human understand the task and each other's roles.
  - Coordination: Coordinating actions and communication between the robot and human.
  - Adaptability: Allowing the robot to adapt to human behavior and preferences.
  - Trust: Building trust between the robot and human.

- Collaboration Scenarios:
  - Shared Workspace: Robots and humans working in the same physical space.
  - Shared Tasks: Robots and humans performing tasks together.
  - Remote Collaboration: Robots and humans collaborating over a distance.

15.2 Implementing Human-Robot Interaction and Collaboration Using ROS and OpenCV

This section outlines the steps involved in implementing a human-robot interaction and collaboration system using ROS and OpenCV.

1. System Architecture:

- Sensors:
  - Camera (for gesture recognition, facial expression recognition, and object tracking).
  - Microphone (for speech recognition).

- Speakers (for speech synthesis).
- Depth sensor (for 3D scene understanding).

- ROS Nodes:
  - Speech Recognition Node: A node that converts human speech into text commands.
  - Speech Synthesis Node: A node that converts text commands into human-like speech.
  - Gesture Recognition Node: A node that interprets human hand gestures.
  - Facial Expression Recognition Node: A node that interprets human facial expressions.
  - Object Tracking Node: A node that tracks objects in the environment.
  - Task Planning Node: A node that coordinates the robot and human's actions.
  - Arm Control Node: A node that controls the robot's robotic arm.
  - Navigation Node: A node that controls the robot's movement.

- OpenCV Integration:
  - Used in the gesture recognition, facial expression recognition, and object tracking nodes for image processing.
  - Used for tasks like feature detection, object detection, and pose estimation.

2. Implementation Steps:
- Sensor Integration:
  - Install and configure ROS drivers for the camera, microphone, and speakers.
  - Publish sensor data as ROS messages.
- Speech Recognition and Synthesis:
  - Use ROS packages like pocketsphinx, google_speech, or vosk for speech recognition.
  - Use ROS packages like festival, espeak_tts, or gtts for speech synthesis.

- Create ROS nodes that subscribe to speech commands and publish speech responses.
- Gesture Recognition:
  - Use OpenCV to process camera images.
  - Implement gesture recognition using techniques like hand tracking and gesture classification.
  - Publish recognized gestures as ROS messages.
- Facial Expression Recognition:
  - Use OpenCV to process camera images.
  - Implement facial expression recognition using deep learning models or traditional image processing techniques.
  - Publish recognized expressions as ROS messages.
- Object Tracking:
  - Use OpenCV to track objects in the environment.

- Implement object tracking algorithms like Kalman filters or correlation tracking.
- Publish object tracking data as ROS messages.
- Task Planning and Coordination:
  - Develop a task planning node that coordinates the robot and human's actions.
  - Use ROS services or actions to manage communication and task execution.
  - Implement feedback mechanisms to ensure shared understanding.
- Arm Control and Navigation:
  - Use ROS control packages to control the robotic arm and robot movement.
  - Integrate arm control and navigation with the task planning node.
- Testing and Evaluation:

- Test the HRI and collaboration system in simulated and real-world scenarios.
- Evaluate the system's performance in terms of communication effectiveness, task efficiency, and user satisfaction.
- Iterate on the design based on user feedback.

3. Example ROS Nodes and Integration:

- Speech Interaction Node:
  - Subscribes to speech command topics.
  - Uses speech recognition to convert speech to text.
  - Uses speech synthesis to generate responses.
  - Publishes robot responses to speech output topics.
- Gesture Recognition Node:
  - Subscribes to camera image topics.

- Uses OpenCV to process images and recognize gestures.
- Publishes recognized gestures as ROS messages.
- Task Coordinator Node:
  - Subscribes to speech commands, gesture recognition, and object tracking topics.
  - Coordinates the robot's actions based on human input and environmental information.
  - Uses ROS services or actions to communicate with arm control and navigation nodes.

This case study demonstrates the practical application of ROS and OpenCV for building a human-robot interaction and collaboration system.

By following these steps and adapting them to specific robot platforms and applications, robotics developers can create robots that can effectively work alongside humans.

Part VI: Advanced Topics and Future Directions

Chapter 16. Deep Learning for Robotics

This chapter explores the application of deep learning techniques to enhance robotic capabilities, particularly in areas like object recognition, tracking, and control. We will cover the introduction to deep learning in a robotic context, and the practical implementation of deep learning for common robotic tasks.

16.1 Introduction to Deep Learning for Robotics

Deep learning, a subset of machine learning, has revolutionized various fields, including computer vision, natural language processing, and robotics.[1] Its ability to learn complex patterns from large datasets makes it highly suitable for addressing challenges in robotics.

Key Concepts:

- Neural Networks: Deep learning models are based on neural networks, which consist of interconnected layers of nodes (neurons).
- Deep Architectures: Deep learning models use multiple layers to learn hierarchical representations of data.
- Backpropagation: An algorithm used to train neural networks by adjusting the weights of connections between neurons.
- Convolutional Neural Networks (CNNs): Neural networks designed for image and video processing.
- Recurrent Neural Networks (RNNs): Neural networks designed for sequential data, such as time series and natural language.
- Reinforcement Learning (RL): A type of machine learning where an agent learns to make decisions by interacting with an environment.[2]
- Transfer Learning: Reusing pre-trained models for new tasks.

Advantages of Deep Learning in Robotics:

- Improved Perception: Deep learning models can achieve high accuracy in object recognition, scene understanding, and sensor data processing.
- Adaptive Control: Deep learning enables robots to learn complex control policies and adapt to changing environments.
- End-to-End Learning: Deep learning allows for end-to-end training, where the robot learns to map raw sensor data to control actions.
- Robustness: Deep learning models can be robust to noise and variations in sensor data.

Challenges of Deep Learning in Robotics:

- Data Requirements: Deep learning models require large amounts of labeled data for training.
- Computational Cost: Training and deploying deep learning models can be computationally expensive.

- Real-Time Performance: Achieving real-time performance can be challenging for complex deep learning models.
- Safety and Reliability: Ensuring the safety and reliability of deep learning-based robotic systems is crucial.
- Generalization: Making models generalize to different environments.
- Explainability: Understanding why a model makes a certain decision.

16.2 Using Deep Learning for Object Recognition, Tracking, and Control

This section explores the practical application of deep learning for common robotic tasks.

Object Recognition:

- Techniques:
  - Image Classification: Identifying the category of an object in an image.
  - Object Detection: Locating and classifying objects within an image.

- Semantic Segmentation: Assigning a semantic label to each pixel in an image.
- Implementation:
  - Use pre-trained CNN models (e.g., ResNet, EfficientNet) for image classification.
  - Use object detection models (e.g., YOLO, SSD, Faster R-CNN) for object localization and classification.
  - Use semantic segmentation models (e.g., U-Net, DeepLab) for pixel-wise classification.
  - Integrate deep learning models with ROS using libraries like torch_ros or tensorflow_ros.
- Applications:
  - Object grasping and manipulation.
  - Scene understanding for navigation.
  - Human-robot interaction.

Object Tracking:

- Techniques:
  - DeepSORT: Combining deep learning-based feature extraction with Kalman filtering for object tracking.
  - Siamese Networks: Learning to compare object features for tracking.
  - Recurrent Neural Networks (RNNs): Modeling the temporal dynamics of object motion.
- Implementation:
  - Use pre-trained deep learning models for feature extraction.
  - Implement Kalman filters or other tracking algorithms.
  - Integrate tracking algorithms with ROS for real-time tracking.
- Applications:
  - Robot navigation in dynamic environments.
  - Human tracking for HRI.
  - Object manipulation in cluttered environments.

Control:

- Techniques:
    - Reinforcement Learning (RL): Training robots to learn control policies through trial and error.
    - Imitation Learning: Learning control policies from human demonstrations.
    - End-to-End Learning: Directly mapping sensor data to control actions using deep neural networks.
- Implementation:
    - Use RL algorithms (e.g., DQN, PPO, SAC) to train control policies.
    - Use imitation learning techniques (e.g., behavioral cloning) to learn from human demonstrations.
    - Use end-to-end deep learning models for mapping sensor data to control actions.
    - Integrate deep learning control with ROS control packages.
- Applications:
    - Robotic grasping and manipulation.

- ○ Autonomous navigation.
- ○ Robotic assembly.

Example: Object Detection with YOLO and ROS:

1. Install YOLO and darknet_ros:
   - ○ Install YOLO and the darknet_ros ROS package.
2. Configure darknet_ros:
   - ○ Download pre-trained YOLO weights and configuration files.
   - ○ Configure the darknet_ros parameters to use the downloaded weights and configuration.
3. Launch darknet_ros:
   - ○ Launch the darknet_ros node to perform object detection.
4. Subscribe to detection results:
   - ○ Create a ROS node that subscribes to the darknet_ros output topic.
   - ○ Process the detection results and use them for robotic tasks.

C++

```cpp
#include <rclcpp/rclcpp.hpp>
#include <darknet_ros_msgs/msg/bounding_boxes.hpp>

class ObjectDetector : public rclcpp::Node {
public:
  ObjectDetector() : Node("object_detector") {
    subscription_ = this->create_subscription<darknet_ros_msgs::msg::BoundingBoxes>(
      "/darknet_ros/bounding_boxes", 10,
      std::bind(&ObjectDetector::detectionCallback, this, std::placeholders::_1));
  }

private:
  void detectionCallback(const darknet_ros_msgs::msg::BoundingBoxes::SharedPtr msg) {
    for (const auto& box : msg->bounding_boxes) {
```

```cpp
            RCLCPP_INFO(this->get_logger(),
"Object:        %s,        x=%d,        y=%d",
box.class_name.c_str(), box.xmin, box.ymin);
        // Process the detection results.
    }
  }


rclcpp::Subscription<darknet_ros_msgs::msg::B
oundingBoxes>::SharedPtr subscription_;
};

int main(int argc, char * argv[]) {
  rclcpp::init(argc, argv);

rclcpp::spin(std::make_shared<ObjectDetector>(
));
  rclcpp::shutdown();
  return 0;
}
```

This chapter provides an introduction to deep learning for robotics and demonstrates its application for object recognition, tracking, and control. By mastering these techniques, robotics developers can create intelligent and adaptive robotic systems.

Chapter 17. Cloud Robotics and IoT

This chapter explores the integration of cloud computing and the Internet of Things (IoT) into robotics, opening up new possibilities for development, deployment, and operation. We will cover the introduction to cloud robotics and IoT, and the practical application of these technologies in robotics.

17.1 Introduction to Cloud Robotics and IoT

Cloud robotics and IoT leverage the power of cloud computing and interconnected devices to enhance robotic capabilities and enable new applications.

Cloud Robotics:

- Concept: Cloud robotics involves using cloud computing resources, such as storage, processing, and networking, to support robotic tasks.

- Benefits:
  - Offloading Computation: Performing computationally intensive tasks (e.g., deep learning, path planning) in the cloud.
  - Data Storage and Analysis: Storing and analyzing large datasets from robots in the cloud.
  - Remote Monitoring and Control: Monitoring and controlling robots remotely through cloud-based interfaces.
  - Software Updates and Deployment: Deploying and updating robot software from the cloud.
  - Collaboration and Sharing: Sharing robot data and algorithms with other robots and users.
- Key Components:
  - Cloud Platforms: Services like AWS, Google Cloud, and Azure providing infrastructure and tools.

- Robotics Middleware: ROS, MQTT, and other communication protocols for connecting robots to the cloud.
- Cloud-Based APIs: APIs for accessing cloud services like machine learning, computer vision, and data analytics.

Internet of Things (IoT):

- Concept: IoT involves connecting physical devices to the internet, enabling them to collect and exchange data.
- Benefits:
  - Sensor Integration: Integrating data from various IoT sensors into robotic systems.
  - Remote Sensing and Monitoring: Monitoring environmental conditions and robot performance remotely.

- Interoperability: Enabling robots to communicate and collaborate with other IoT devices.
  - Data-Driven Decision Making: Using IoT data to optimize robot behavior and performance.
- Key Components:
  - IoT Devices: Sensors, actuators, and other devices connected to the internet.
  - IoT Platforms: Services for managing and processing IoT data.
  - Communication Protocols: MQTT, CoAP, and other protocols for IoT communication.

17.2 Using Cloud Robotics and IoT for Robotics Development and Deployment

This section explores the practical application of cloud robotics and IoT in robotics development and deployment.

Development:

- Simulation and Testing: Using cloud-based simulation environments (e.g., Gazebo in the cloud) for robot development and testing.
- Data Collection and Labeling: Storing and labeling large datasets from robots in the cloud for training machine learning models.
- Model Training and Deployment: Training and deploying deep learning models in the cloud for object recognition, control, and other tasks.
- Software Development and Deployment: Using cloud-based development tools and continuous integration/continuous deployment (CI/CD) pipelines for robot software development.
- Remote Debugging and Monitoring: Debugging and monitoring robots remotely through cloud-based tools.

Deployment:

- Remote Monitoring and Control: Monitoring and controlling robots remotely through cloud-based interfaces.
- Data Logging and Analysis: Logging and analyzing robot data in the cloud for performance optimization and fault detection.
- Over-the-Air (OTA) Updates: Deploying software updates and patches to robots remotely.
- Fleet Management: Managing and coordinating fleets of robots through cloud-based platforms.
- Cloud-Based Navigation and Mapping: Using cloud-based services for navigation and mapping in large-scale environments.
- Collaborative Robotics: Enabling robots to collaborate with other robots and humans through cloud-based communication and coordination.
- Edge Computing: Processing data at the edge of the network to reduce latency and bandwidth usage.

- Robots as a Service (RaaS): Providing robotic services through cloud-based platforms.

Example: Cloud-Based Object Recognition:

1. Robot Captures Image:
   - A robot captures an image using its camera.
2. Image Upload to Cloud:
   - The robot uploads the image to a cloud storage service (e.g., AWS S3, Google Cloud Storage).
3. Cloud-Based Object Recognition:
   - A cloud-based object recognition service (e.g., Google Cloud Vision API, AWS Rekognition) processes the image.
4. Detection Results Sent to Robot:
   - The cloud service sends the object detection results back to the robot.
5. Robot Acts on Results:
   - The robot uses the object detection results for tasks like grasping, navigation, or interaction.

Example IoT Integration:

1. Environmental Monitoring:
   - IoT sensors (e.g., temperature, humidity, light) collect environmental data.
2. Data Sent to IoT Platform:
   - The IoT sensors send data to an IoT platform (e.g., AWS IoT, Azure IoT).
3. Data Processed and Analyzed:
   - The IoT platform processes and analyzes the sensor data.
4. Robot Receives Data:
   - The robot receives the processed data from the IoT platform.
5. Robot Acts on Data:
   - The robot adjusts its behavior based on the environmental data (e.g., adjusts its speed, activates a fan).

This chapter provides an overview of cloud robotics and IoT, and demonstrates their application in robotics development and deployment.

By leveraging these technologies, robotics developers can create more powerful, scalable, and intelligent robotic systems.

Chapter 18. Future Directions in Robotics Development

This chapter explores the exciting and rapidly evolving landscape of robotics development, highlighting emerging trends and technologies that are shaping the future of the field.

18.1 Overview of Future Directions in Robotics Development

The field of robotics is undergoing a profound transformation, driven by advancements in artificial intelligence, materials science, and computing. Future robots are expected to be more intelligent, adaptablc, and capable of operating in complex and dynamic environments.

Key Drivers of Future Robotics Development:

- Artificial Intelligence (AI): AI is enabling robots to perceive, reason, and learn, leading to more autonomous and intelligent systems.
- Machine Learning (ML) and Deep Learning (DL): ML and DL are enabling robots to learn from data, improving their ability to adapt and perform complex tasks.
- Computer Vision: Advanced computer vision techniques are enabling robots to perceive and understand their surroundings with greater accuracy and detail.
- Sensor Fusion: Combining data from multiple sensors is improving the accuracy and robustness of robot perception.
- Cloud Robotics and IoT: Connecting robots to the cloud and IoT is enabling remote monitoring, control, and data sharing.

- Edge Computing: Processing data at the edge of the network is reducing latency and improving real-time performance.
- Materials Science: Advancements in materials science are leading to the development of more flexible, durable, and lightweight robots.
- Human-Robot Interaction (HRI): Improved HRI is enabling robots to interact with humans in a more natural and intuitive way.
- Robotics Simulation: Advanced simulation tools are enabling faster development and testing of robotic systems.
- Open-Source Robotics: The open-source robotics community is fostering collaboration and innovation.

18.2 Emerging Trends and Technologies in Robotics Development

This section explores some of the most prominent emerging trends and technologies that are shaping the future of robotics development.

1. Cognitive Robotics:

- Focuses on developing robots with cognitive abilities, such as reasoning, planning, and problem-solving.
- Integrates AI techniques like knowledge representation, planning, and learning.
- Enables robots to perform complex tasks in unstructured environments.

2. Soft Robotics:

- Uses flexible and deformable materials to create robots that can adapt to their environment.
- Enables robots to perform tasks that are difficult for traditional rigid robots, such as grasping delicate objects and navigating confined spaces.
- Inspired by biological systems, such as octopus tentacles and elephant trunks.

3. Collaborative Robots (Cobots):

- Designed to work alongside humans in shared workspaces.
- Equipped with safety features, such as collision detection and force control.
- Used in manufacturing, logistics, and other industries to improve productivity and efficiency.

4. Swarm Robotics:

- Involves coordinating the actions of a large number of simple robots to achieve a common goal.
- Inspired by biological systems, such as ant colonies and bird flocks.
- Used in applications such as search and rescue, environmental monitoring, and construction.

5. Bio-Inspired Robotics:

- Draws inspiration from biological systems to design and develop robots.

- Enables robots to perform tasks that are difficult for traditional robots, such as walking on uneven terrain and swimming.
- Examples include legged robots inspired by animals and underwater robots inspired by fish.

6. Micro and Nano Robotics:

- Focuses on developing robots at the micro and nanoscale.
- Enables robots to perform tasks in confined spaces, such as inside the human body.
- Used in applications such as drug delivery, medical imaging, and environmental monitoring.

7. Digital Twins in Robotics:

- Creating virtual representations of physical robots.
- Used for simulation, testing, and optimization of robotic systems.

- Enables remote monitoring and control of robots.

8. Federated Learning in Robotics:

- Training machine learning models on decentralized data from multiple robots.
- Enables robots to learn from each other without sharing sensitive data.
- Improves the robustness and generalization of robotic systems.

9. Explainable AI (XAI) in Robotics:

- Developing AI models that can explain their decisions and actions.
- Improves the transparency and trustworthiness of robotic systems.
- Crucial for safety-critical applications.

10. Ethical Robotics:

- Addressing the ethical implications of robotics development and deployment.

- Developing guidelines and standards for responsible robotics research and innovation.
- Ensuring that robots are used for the benefit of humanity.

The future of robotics development is filled with exciting possibilities. By embracing these emerging trends and technologies, robotics developers can create intelligent, adaptable, and beneficial robotic systems that will transform various industries and improve our lives.

Conclusion: Navigating the Frontier of Robotics Development

This comprehensive exploration into C++ and its application within the realm of robotics has traversed a multifaceted landscape, from the foundational principles of the language itself to the cutting-edge frontiers of AI-driven robotic systems. We've journeyed through the intricacies of C++ fundamentals, the power of the Standard Template Library, the visual prowess of OpenCV, and the collaborative framework of ROS. We've also delved into the practicalities of sensor integration, motion planning, and human-robot interaction, culminating in case studies that illustrate the real-world implementation of these concepts.

Recapitulation of Key Learnings:

- C++ as a Cornerstone: C++'s performance, low-level control, and robust object-oriented capabilities render it an indispensable tool for robotics development, particularly in real-time and embedded systems.
- STL's Efficiency: The Standard Template Library significantly streamlines development by providing efficient data structures and algorithms, optimizing code for performance-critical applications.
- OpenCV's Visual Perception: OpenCV empowers robots with the ability to "see" and interpret their environment, enabling tasks like object detection, tracking, and navigation.
- ROS's Collaborative Framework: ROS fosters modularity and interoperability, facilitating the development of complex robotic systems through its distributed computing and message-passing architecture.
- Sensor Fusion and Data Processing: The integration and processing of sensor data

are crucial for creating robust and reliable robotic systems, requiring techniques like filtering and sensor fusion.

- Motion Planning and Control: Algorithms like A* and D*, along with control techniques like PID and MPC, are essential for enabling robots to navigate and manipulate objects effectively.
- Human-Robot Interaction (HRI): Designing intuitive and safe interfaces is paramount for enabling seamless collaboration between humans and robots.
- Deep Learning's Transformative Power: Deep learning is revolutionizing robotics by enabling robots to learn complex patterns and perform tasks with unprecedented accuracy.
- Cloud Robotics and IoT's Scalability: Cloud computing and the Internet of Things are expanding the horizons of robotics, enabling remote monitoring, data analysis, and collaborative operations.

The Evolving Landscape of Robotics:

The field of robotics is in a state of constant evolution, driven by advancements in artificial intelligence, sensor technology, and materials science. Emerging trends like cognitive robotics, soft robotics, and swarm robotics are pushing the boundaries of what's possible. The integration of digital twins, federated learning, and explainable AI is also shaping the future of robotics development.

Looking Ahead:

The future of robotics holds immense potential, with robots poised to play increasingly significant roles in various aspects of our lives. As we move forward, it's crucial to address the ethical implications of robotics development, ensuring that these technologies are used responsibly and for the benefit of humanity.

Key areas that will define the future of Robotics:

- Enhanced Autonomy: Robots will exhibit greater autonomy, capable of operating in complex and dynamic environments without human intervention.

- Improved Human-Robot Collaboration: Robots will seamlessly collaborate with humans, working alongside them to achieve shared goals.
- Advanced Perception and Cognition: Robots will possess advanced perception and cognitive abilities, enabling them to understand and interact with their surroundings more intelligently.
- Ubiquitous Robotics: Robots will become more prevalent in various industries and everyday life, from manufacturing and healthcare to transportation and entertainment.
- Sustainable Robotics: Development of robots that are energy efficient, and use sustainable materials.
- Increased Safety and Security: Continued development of safety protocols, and security measures to protect both humans and robots.

A Call to Innovation:

The challenges and opportunities in robotics development are vast and exciting. By embracing innovation, collaboration, and ethical considerations, we can harness the transformative power of robotics to create a better future for all.

This comprehensive guide serves as a foundation for those venturing into the dynamic realm of robotics. It highlights the importance of mastering fundamental tools like C++, and adapting to the rapid advancements that are shaping the future. The field awaits those who are ready to contribute to its growth, and push the boundaries of robotic capabilities.

Appendices

This section provides supplementary material to enhance understanding and facilitate further exploration of the topics covered in this book. These appendices offer valuable resources, code examples, and detailed explanations of specific concepts, serving as a practical guide for robotics developers.

Appendix A: C++ Language Reference

This appendix provides a concise reference for key C++ language features, including syntax, data types, operators, and control structures.

- A.1: Data Types and Variables:
  - Detailed description of primitive data types (int, float, double, char, bool) and their modifiers.
  - Explanation of variable declaration, initialization, and scope.

- Examples of using different data
  types and variables.
- A.2: Operators and Expressions:
  - Comprehensive overview of
    arithmetic, assignment, comparison,
    logical, bitwise, and other
    operators.
  - Explanation of operator precedence
    and associativity.
  - Examples of using operators in
    expressions.
- A.3: Control Structures:
  - Detailed explanation of if, if-else,
    switch, for, while, and do-while
    statements.
  - Examples of using control
    structures to control program flow.
  - Explanation of break, continue, and
    return statements.
- A.4: Functions:
  - Explanation of function declaration,
    definition, and calling.
  - Examples of using functions with
    parameters and return values.

- Explanation of function overloading and recursion.
- A.5: Object-Oriented Programming (OOP):
  - Detailed explanation of classes, objects, encapsulation, inheritance, and polymorphism.
  - Examples of defining and using classes and objects.
  - Explanation of constructors, destructors, and access specifiers.
- A.6: Pointers and Memory Management:
  - Explanation of pointers, dynamic memory allocation, and deallocation.
  - Examples of using pointers to access and manipulate memory.
  - Discussion of memory leaks and best practices for memory management.

Appendix B: STL Container and Algorithm Reference

This appendix provides a reference for commonly used STL containers and algorithms, with examples and explanations.

- B.1: std::vector:
  - Detailed explanation of std::vector functionality and usage.
  - Examples of using std::vector for storing and manipulating data.
- B.2: std::list and std::deque:
  - Detailed explanation of std::list and std::deque functionality and usage.
  - Examples of using these containers for different applications.
- B.3: std::map and std::set:
  - Detailed explanation of std::map and std::set functionality and usage.
  - Examples of using these containers for storing and retrieving data.
- B.4: STL Algorithms:
  - Explanation of commonly used STL algorithms (sort, find, transform, accumulate, copy).
  - Examples of using these algorithms with different containers.

- B.5: Iterators:
    - Explanation of the different types of iterators, and their usage.
    - Examples of using iterators to traverse containers.

Appendix C: OpenCV Function Reference

This appendix provides a reference for commonly used OpenCV functions, with examples and explanations.

- C.1: Image Loading and Saving:
    - Detailed explanation of cv::imread() and cv::imwrite() functions.
    - Examples of loading and saving images in different formats.
- C.2: Image Filtering and Thresholding:
    - Explanation of cv::blur(), cv::GaussianBlur(), cv::medianBlur(), cv::threshold(), and cv::adaptiveThreshold() functions.

- Examples of applying different filtering and thresholding techniques.
- C.3: Image Transformations and Feature Detection:
  - Explanation of cv::resize(), cv::warpAffine(), cv::warpPerspective(), cv::cvtColor(), cv::cornerHarris(), and cv::Canny().
  - Explanation of feature detectors like ORB, SIFT, and SURF.
  - Examples of applying image transformations and feature detection techniques.
- C.4: Object Detection:
  - Examples of using Haar Cascades, and deep learning models for object detection within OpenCV.

Appendix D: ROS Message and Service Definitions

This appendix provides a reference for commonly used ROS message and service definitions, with examples and explanations.

- D.1: Standard ROS Messages:
    - Explanation of commonly used standard ROS messages (std_msgs, sensor_msgs, geometry_msgs).
    - Examples of using these messages in ROS nodes.
- D.2: Creating Custom Messages and Services:
    - Explanation of creating custom ROS messages and services using .msg and .srv files.
    - Examples of defining and using custom messages and services.

Appendix E: ROS Navigation and Mapping Configuration

This appendix provides configuration examples and explanations for ROS navigation and mapping tools.

- E.1: gmapping Configuration:
  - Explanation of key gmapping parameters and their effects.
  - Example gmapping launch file.
- E.2: amcl Configuration:
  - Explanation of key amcl parameters and their effects.
  - Example amcl configuration file.
- E.3: move_base Configuration:
  - Explanation of key move_base parameters and their effects.
  - Explanation of costmap configuration.
  - Example move_base configuration files.

Appendix F: Deep Learning Libraries and Tools

This appendix provides a reference for commonly used deep learning libraries and tools, with examples and explanations.

- F.1: TensorFlow and Keras:

- Explanation of TensorFlow and Keras functionalities and usage.
- Examples of building and training deep learning models.
- F.2: PyTorch:
  - Explanation of PyTorch functionalities and usage.
  - Examples of building and training deep learning models.
- F.3: ROS Integration:
  - Examples of integrating Tensorflow and Pytorch with ROS.

These appendices serve as valuable resources for robotics developers, providing detailed information and practical examples to support the implementation and development of robotic systems.

Index

- *A Algorithm*
  - Path planning
  - Graph search
  - Heuristic function
  - Optimal path
- **Abstraction (OOP)**
  - Hiding complexity
  - Interface design
  - Simplified usage
- **Access Specifiers (OOP)**
  - Public
  - Private
  - Protected
- **Actionlib (ROS)**
  - Long-running tasks
  - Feedback and results

- o Goal-oriented communication
- **Adaptive Thresholding (OpenCV)**
  - o Image processing
  - o Variable threshold
  - o Local neighborhood
- **Algorithms (STL)**
  - o Sorting
  - o Searching
  - o Transforming
  - o Accumulating
- **AKAZE**
  - o Feature detection
  - o Feature descriptor
  - o Image processing
- **AMCL (ROS)**
  - o Localization
  - o Adaptive Monte Carlo Localization
  - o Particle filter
- **Arrays (C++)**
  - o Declaration
  - o Initialization
  - o Accessing elements
  - o Multidimensional arrays
- **Artificial Intelligence (AI)**

- Robotics
- Cognitive abilities
- Decision making
- **Augmented Reality (AR) Interfaces**
  - Human-robot interaction
  - Overlaying information
  - Enhanced interaction
- **Autonomous Navigation**
  - Robot movement
  - Path planning
  - Obstacle avoidance
- **B-Splines**
  - Path planning
  - Smooth trajectories
  - Robotics control
- **Backpropagation**
  - Deep learning
  - Neural network training
  - Weight adjustment
- **Base Classes (OOP)**
  - Inheritance
  - Code reusability
  - Hierarchical design
- **BFMatcher (OpenCV)**

- Feature matching
- Brute-force approach
- Image processing
- **Bio-Inspired Robotics**
  - Nature-inspired design
  - Adaptability
  - Advanced locomotion
- **Bitwise Operators (C++)**
  - Binary operations
  - Data manipulation
  - Low-level control
- **BRISK**
  - Feature detection
  - Feature descriptor
  - Image processing
- **C++**
  - Programming language
  - Performance
  - Low-level control
  - Object-oriented programming
- **C++11/14/17/20/23**
  - Modern C++
  - Language evolution
  - New features

- **Camera Calibration (OpenCV)**
  - Image processing
  - Intrinsic parameters
  - Extrinsic parameters
- **Cartographer (ROS)**
  - SLAM
  - Mapping
  - Robotics navigation
- **Cascade Classifier (OpenCV)**
  - Object detection
  - Haar-like features
  - Machine learning
- **Classes (OOP)**
  - Blueprints
  - Attributes
  - Behaviors
- **CLion**
  - IDE
  - C++ development
  - Robotics
- **Cloud Platforms**
  - AWS
  - Google Cloud
  - Azure

- ○ Cloud robotics
- **Cloud Robotics**
  - ○ Robotics
  - ○ Cloud computing
  - ○ Remote operation
- **CMake**
  - ○ Build system
  - ○ C++ projects
  - ○ OpenCV
- **CMakeLists.txt**
  - ○ CMake configuration file
  - ○ Build instructions
  - ○ Dependencies
- **CLion**
  - ○ IDE
  - ○ C++ development
  - ○ Robotics
- **Cognitive Robotics**
  - ○ Robotics
  - ○ Artificial intelligence
  - ○ Reasoning and planning
- **Color Spaces (OpenCV)**
  - ○ Image processing
  - ○ RGB

- ○ HSV
- ○ Grayscale
- **Compile-time Polymorphism (OOP)**
  - ○ Function overloading
  - ○ Operator overloading
  - ○ Static binding
- **Containers (STL)**
  - ○ Data structures
  - ○ Vectors
  - ○ Lists
  - ○ Maps
- **Control Structures (C++)**
  - ○ If statements
  - ○ For loops
  - ○ While loops
- **Constructors (OOP)**
  - ○ Object initialization
  - ○ Member variables
  - ○ Default constructor
- **Coroutines (C++20)**
  - ○ Asynchronous programming
  - ○ Concurrency
  - ○ Efficient execution
- **Costmap_2d (ROS)**

- Navigation
- Cost mapping
- Obstacle avoidance
- *D Algorithm**
  - Path planning
  - Dynamic environments
  - Replanning
- **Data Association**
  - Sensor fusion
  - Object tracking
  - Robotics perception
- **Data Types (C++)**
  - Int
  - Float
  - Double
  - Char
  - Bool
- **Deducing this (C++23)**
  - Object-oriented programming
  - Member functions
  - Flexibility
- **Deep Learning**
  - Machine learning
  - Neural networks

- Robotics
- **DeepLab**
  - Semantic segmentation
  - Image processing
  - Robotics vision
- **DeepSORT**
  - Object tracking
  - Deep learning
  - Robotics
- **Deque (STL)**
  - Double-ended queue
  - Efficient insertion/deletion
  - Robotics data management
- **Derived Classes (OOP)**
  - Inheritance
  - Extending functionality
  - Specialization
- **Destructors (OOP)**
  - Object cleanup
  - Resource release
  - Memory management
- **Digital Twins**
  - Robotics
  - Virtual representation

- Simulation and control
- **DQN**
  - Reinforcement learning
  - Robotics control
  - Q-learning
- **DWA (Dynamic Window Approach)**
  - Local path planning
  - Robotics navigation
  - Real-time control
- **Edge Computing**
  - Robotics
  - Data processing
  - Reduced latency
- **Eigen**
  - C++ library
  - Linear algebra
  - Robotics
- **Encapsulation (OOP)**
  - Data hiding
  - Information protection
  - Modularity
- **End-to-End Learning**
  - Deep learning
  - Robotics control

- o Direct mapping
- **Espeak_tts (ROS)**
  - o Speech synthesis
  - o Text-to-speech
  - o Human-robot interaction
- **Ethical Robotics**
  - o Responsible development
  - o Social impact
  - o Safety and trust
- **Explainable AI (XAI)**
  - o Robotics
  - o Transparency
  - o Decision making
- **Facial Expression Recognition**
  - o Human-robot interaction
  - o Emotion detection
  - o Computer vision
- **Federated Learning**
  - o Robotics
  - o Distributed learning
  - o Data privacy
- **Festival (ROS)**
  - o Speech synthesis
  - o Text-to-speech

- o Human-robot interaction
- **Feature Detection (OpenCV)**
  - o Image processing
  - o Corner detection
  - o Edge detection
- **Feature Matching (OpenCV)**
  - o Image processing
  - o Image stitching
  - o Object recognition
- **Filtering (Signal Processing)**
  - o Noise reduction
  - o Data smoothing
  - o Sensor data
- **FlannBasedMatcher (OpenCV)**
  - o Feature matching
  - o Approximate Nearest Neighbors
  - o Image processing
- **For_each (STL)**
  - o Algorithm
  - o Iteration
  - o Function application
- **Function Overloading (C++)**
  - o Multiple functions
  - o Same name

- o Different parameters
- **Functions (C++)**
  - o Declaration
  - o Definition
  - o Calling
  - o Parameters
  - o Return values
- **Gazebo**
  - o Robotics simulator
  - o ROS integration
  - o Testing and development
- **Geometric Transformations (OpenCV)**
  - o Image processing
  - o Rotation
  - o Translation
  - o Scaling
- **Gesture Recognition**
  - o Human-robot interaction
  - o Hand tracking
  - o Command interpretation
- **Global Planning**
  - o Path planning
  - o Complete environment
  - o Robotics navigation

- **Gmapping (ROS)**
  - SLAM
  - Mapping
  - Robotics navigation
- **Google Cloud**
  - Cloud platform
  - Robotics services
  - Data storage
- **Google Speech (ROS)**
  - Speech recognition
  - Cloud API
  - Human-robot interaction
- **GOTO Statement (C++)**
  - Jump statement
  - Control flow
  - Generally discouraged
- **GPose Estimation**
  - Computer vision
  - Robotics
  - Object pose estimation
- **GPTS (Google Text-to-Speech)**
  - Text-to-speech
  - Human-robot interaction
  - Cloud API

- **Graphical User Interfaces (GUIs)**
  - Human-robot interaction
  - Visual displays
  - Interactive controls
- **Haar Cascades (OpenCV)**
  - Object detection
  - Face detection
  - Machine learning
- **Hardware Abstraction (ROS)**
  - Device independence
  - Sensor drivers
  - Actuator control
- **Hector_slam (ROS)**
  - SLAM
  - Mapping
  - Odometry-free
- **HRI Modalities**
  - Visual communication
  - Auditory communication
  - Tactile communication
- **HSV (Hue, Saturation, Value)**
  - Color space
  - Image processing
  - Color representation

- **Human-Robot Collaboration**
  - Shared workspace
  - Task coordination
  - Robot assistance
- **Human-Robot Interaction (HRI)**
  - Robot communication
  - User interfaces
  - Social aspects
- **If Consteval (C++23)**
  - Compile-time execution
  - Conditional statements
  - Performance optimization
- **If-Else Statement (C++)**
  - Conditional execution
  - Alternative branches
  - Program flow
- **Image Filtering (OpenCV)**
  - Blurring
  - Sharpening
  - Noise reduction
- **Image Processing (OpenCV)**
  - Image manipulation
  - Feature extraction
  - Robotics vision

- **Image Segmentation (OpenCV)**
  - Pixel labeling
  - Object isolation
  - Robotics scene understanding
- **Image Transformations (OpenCV)**
  - Resizing
  - Rotation
  - Warping
- **IMU (Inertial Measurement Unit)**
  - Sensor
  - Acceleration
  - Angular velocity
- **Inheritance (OOP)**
  - Code reuse
  - Class hierarchy
  - Derived classes
- **InputArray (OpenCV)**
  - Image data type
  - Function arguments
  - Flexibility
- **IoT Devices**
  - Sensors
  - Actuators
  - Connected devices

- **IoT Platforms**
  - Data management
  - Device communication
  - Cloud services
- **Iterators (STL)**
  - Container access
  - Traversal
  - Algorithms
- **Kalman Filter**
  - State estimation
  - Noise reduction
  - Object tracking
- **Keras**
  - Deep learning library
  - TensorFlow
  - Robotics applications
- **Lambda Expressions (C++11)**
  - Anonymous functions
  - Concise syntax
  - STL algorithms
- **Laplacian (OpenCV)**
  - Edge detection
  - Image processing
  - Robotics vision

- **Lidar**
  - Sensor
  - Range sensing
  - 3D mapping
- **List (STL)**
  - Doubly linked list
  - Efficient insertion/deletion
  - Robotics data management
- **Local Planning**
  - Path planning
  - Limited area
  - Robotics navigation
- **Localization (Robotics)**
  - Pose estimation
  - Robot position
  - Navigation
- **Logical Operators (C++)**
  - Boolean logic
  - Conditional statements
  - Program flow
- **Long Long (C++)**
  - Integer data type
  - Large values
  - Robotics calculations

- **Low-Level Control (C++)**
  - Hardware access
  - Memory management
  - Real-time systems
- **Machine Learning (ML)**
  - Robotics
  - Pattern recognition
  - Data analysis
- **Map (STL)**
  - Associative container
  - Key-value pairs
  - Robotics data management
- **Map_server (ROS)**
  - Navigation
  - Map loading
  - Map serving
- **Map_saver (ROS)**
  - Navigation
  - Map saving
  - Map management
- **Mapping (Robotics)**
  - Environment representation
  - Occupancy grid
  - SLAM

- **Mat (OpenCV)**
  - Matrix class
  - Image data
  - Data storage
- **Mean Shift Tracking**
  - Object tracking
  - Image processing
  - Robotics vision
- **Median Filter (OpenCV)**
  - Noise reduction
  - Image processing
  - Robotics vision
- **Messages (ROS)**
  - Data structures
  - Topic communication
  - Node interaction
- **Micro and Nano Robotics**
  - Small-scale robots
  - Medical applications
  - Targeted interventions
- **MinGW**
  - C++ compiler
  - Windows environment
  - Robotics development

- **Model Predictive Control (MPC)**
  - Robotics control
  - Optimization
  - Predictive behavior
- **Modules (C++20)**
  - Code organization
  - Improved compilation
  - Dependency management
- **Motion Control (Robotics)**
  - Actuator control
  - Trajectory following
  - Robot movement
- **Motion Planning (Robotics)**
  - Path generation
  - Obstacle avoidance
  - Robotics navigation
- **Move_base (ROS)**
  - Navigation
  - Path planning
  - Motion control
- **MSVC (Microsoft Visual C++)**
  - C++ compiler
  - Windows environment
  - Robotics development

- **MQTT**
  - Messaging protocol
  - IoT communication
  - Robotics data transfer
- **Multidimensional Arrays (C++)**
  - Arrays of arrays
  - Matrix representation
  - Robotics data storage
- **Namespaces (C++)**
  - Code organization
  - Name collisions
  - Scope resolution
- **Navigation (Robotics)**
  - Autonomous movement
  - Path planning
  - Localization
- **NMEA_navsat_driver (ROS)**
  - GPS interface
  - Navigation
  - Sensor integration
- **Nodes (ROS)**
  - Executable processes
  - ROS communication
  - Modular design

- **Object Detection (OpenCV)**
  - Image processing
  - Object localization
  - Robotics vision
- **Object-Oriented Programming (OOP)**
  - Classes
  - Objects
  - Inheritance
  - Polymorphism
- **Objects (OOP)**
  - Instances of classes
  - Data and methods
  - Real-world entities
- **Occupancy Grid Maps**
  - Robotics mapping
  - Environment representation
  - Navigation
- **Odometry**
  - Robot motion
  - Position estimation
  - Wheel encoders
- **Open Source**
  - Software availability
  - Community collaboration

- o Robotics development
- **OpenCV**
  - o Computer vision library
  - o Image processing
  - o Robotics vision
- **Operator Overloading (C++)**
  - o Custom operator behavior
  - o Class objects
  - o Intuitive syntax
- **Operators (C++)**
  - o Arithmetic operators
  - o Assignment operators
  - o Comparison operators
  - o Logical operators
- **Optical Flow**
  - o Motion estimation
  - o Video analysis
  - o Robotics vision
- **ORB**
  - o Feature detection
  - o Feature descriptor
  - o Image processing
- **OutputArray (OpenCV)**
  - o Image data type

- ○ Function arguments
- ○ Flexibility
- **Over-the-Air (OTA) Updates**
  - ○ Software deployment
  - ○ Remote updates
  - ○ Robotics systems
- **Parameters (ROS)**
  - ○ Configuration values
  - ○ Node settings
  - ○ Parameter server
- **Particle Filters**
  - ○ State estimation
  - ○ Nonlinear systems
  - ○ Object tracking
- **Path Planning (Robotics)**
  - ○ Trajectory generation
  - ○ Obstacle avoidance
  - ○ Robotics navigation
- **PCL (Point Cloud Library)**
  - ○ 3D data processing
  - ○ Robotics perception
  - ○ Point cloud manipulation
- **Perception (Robotics)**
  - ○ Sensor data

- Environment understanding
- Robot awareness
- **PID Controllers**
  - Robotics control
  - Feedback control
  - Error correction
- **Pocketsphinx (ROS)**
  - Speech recognition
  - Offline processing
  - Human-robot interaction
- **Polymorphism (OOP)**
  - Multiple forms
  - Dynamic binding
  - Flexibility
- **PPO**
  - Reinforcement learning
  - Robotics control
  - Policy optimization
- **Qt Creator**
  - IDE
  - C++ development
  - Robotics
- **RANSAC**
  - Robust estimation

- ○ Outlier removal
- ○ Robotics perception
- **RCLCPP**
  - ○ ROS C++ client library
  - ○ Node creation
  - ○ Communication
- **RQT (ROS)**
  - ○ GUI framework
  - ○ Visualization
  - ○ Monitoring
- **RRT (Rapidly-exploring Random Tree)**
  - ○ Path planning
  - ○ Sampling-based algorithm
  - ○ Robotics navigation
- **Rviz (ROS)**
  - ○ 3D visualization
  - ○ Robot models
  - ○ Sensor data
- **Robotics**
  - ○ Automation
  - ○ Intelligent machines
  - ○ Diverse applications
- **Robotics Middleware**
  - ○ ROS

- ○ Communication protocols
- ○ Software framework
- **ROS (Robot Operating System)**
  - ○ Robotics framework
  - ○ Message passing
  - ○ Tools and libraries
- **ROS Control**
  - ○ Robot control
  - ○ Hardware interface
  - ○ Joint control
- **ROS2**
  - ○ Next-generation ROS
  - ○ Improved performance
  - ○ Real-time capabilities
- **Rostopic**
  - ○ ROS command-line tool
  - ○ Topic interaction
  - ○ Data inspection
- **Run-time Polymorphism (OOP)**
  - ○ Virtual functions
  - ○ Dynamic binding
  - ○ Inheritance
- **SAC**
  - ○ Reinforcement learning

- ○ Robotics control
- ○ Soft Actor-Critic
- **Scene Understanding**
  - ○ Robotics perception
  - ○ Environment interpretation
  - ○ Contextual awareness
- **Sensor Fusion**
  - ○ Data integration
  - ○ Improved accuracy
  - ○ Robotics perception
- **Sensor_msgs (ROS)**
  - ○ ROS message package
  - ○ Sensor data formats
  - ○ Standard messages
- **Sensors (Robotics)**
  - ○ Cameras
  - ○ Lidar
  - ○ IMU
  - ○ GPS
- **Set (STL)**
  - ○ Sorted collection
  - ○ Unique elements
  - ○ Robotics data management
- **Shared Pointers (C++11)**

- Smart pointers
- Memory management
- Resource ownership
- **SIFT**
  - Feature detection
  - Feature descriptor
  - Image processing
- **SLAM (Simultaneous Localization and Mapping)**
  - Robot navigation
  - Map building
  - Pose estimation
- **Smart Pointers (C++11)**
  - Memory management
  - Automatic deallocation
  - Resource safety
- **Social Acceptability**
  - Human-robot interaction
  - Robot appearance
  - Behavior
- **Soft Robotics**
  - Flexible robots
  - Adaptive manipulation
  - Bio-inspired design

- **Sobel (OpenCV)**
  - Edge detection
  - Image processing
  - Robotics vision
- **Speech Recognition**
  - Voice input
  - Command interpretation
  - Human-robot interaction
- **Speech Synthesis**
  - Voice output
  - Text-to-speech
  - Human-robot interaction
- **SSD**
  - Object detection
  - Deep learning
  - Real-time performance
- **Standard Template Library (STL)**
  - C++ library
  - Containers
  - Algorithms
  - Iterators
- **State Estimation**
  - Robot pose
  - Sensor data

- o Filtering
- **Static Mapping**
  - o Map building
  - o Stationary environment
  - o Robotics navigation
- **Structured Bindings (C++17)**
  - o Tuple unpacking
  - o Improved readability
  - o Robotics data access
- **SURF**
  - o Feature detection
  - o Feature descriptor
  - o Image processing
- **Swarm Robotics**
  - o Multi-robot systems
  - o Cooperative behavior
  - o Distributed tasks
- **Switch Statement (C++)**
  - o Multi-way branching
  - o Value selection
  - o Program flow
- **TensorFlow**
  - o Deep learning library
  - o Robotics applications

- o GPU acceleration
- **Ternary Operator (C++)**
  - o Conditional expression
  - o Concise syntax
  - o Program flow
- **TEB (Timed-Elastic-Band)**
  - o Local path planning
  - o Robotics navigation
  - o Trajectory optimization
- **Thresholding (OpenCV)**
  - o Image segmentation
  - o Binary images
  - o Object isolation
- **Topics (ROS)**
  - o Data channels
  - o Publish/subscribe
  - o Asynchronous communication
- **Transform (STL)**
  - o Algorithm
  - o Function application
  - o Data modification
- **Virtual Functions (OOP)**
  - o Dynamic dispatch
  - o Run-time polymorphism

- ○ Inheritance
- **Visual Studio Code (VS Code)**
  - ○ Code editor
  - ○ C++ support
  - ○ Robotics development
- **Vosk**
  - ○ Speech recognition
  - ○ Offline processing
  - ○ Human-robot interaction
- **WarpAffine (OpenCV)**
  - ○ Image transformation
  - ○ Affine transformation
  - ○ Robotics vision
- **WarpPerspective (OpenCV)**
  - ○ Image transformation
  - ○ Perspective transformation
  - ○ Robotics vision
- **While Loop (C++)**
  - ○ Iterative execution
  - ○ Condition checking
  - ○ Program flow
- **WSL (Windows Subsystem for Linux)**
  - ○ Linux environment
  - ○ Windows

- ○ ROS development
- **YOLO**
  - ○ Object detection
  - ○ Deep learning
  - ○ Real-time performance